Michigan Wildlife Viewing Guide

Author
Phil T. Seng

Project Managers
David J. Case and Phil T. Seng, D.J. Case & Associates
Raymond Rustem, Michigan DNR Wildlife Division

A cooperative project initiated by the
Michigan Department of Natural Resources
Wildlife Division
Natural Heritage Program

DNR

Michigan State University Press
East Lansing
1994

Acknowledgements

Steering Committee

The following people served on the *Michigan Wildlife Viewing Guide* Steering Committee. They provided technical expertise and invaluable guidance throughout the duration of the project.

Michigan Department of Natural Resources
    Raymond Rustem, Wildlife Division
    Ned Fogle, Fisheries Division
    Ron Nagel, Parks and Recreation Division
    Ted Reuschel, Forest Management Division
Chuck Budd, Michigan Travel Bureau
Gary Dawson, Consumers Power Company
Ed DeVries and Denise Johnston, Shiawassee National Wildlife Refuge
Jerry Edde, Ottawa National Forest
Rex Ennis and Gloria Boersma, Huron-Manistee National Forests
Sean Harrington, Harrington & Fish Design
Greg Huntington, Michigan Department of Military Affairs
Ray Kimpel, Sleeping Bear Dunes National Lakeshore
Dennis Knapp, Michigan United Conservation Clubs
Dave Kronk and Gregg Bruff, Pictured Rocks National Lakeshore
Dick Lehman, Michigan Audubon Society
Julie Loehr, Michigan State University Press
Ronald McIntyre, Detroit Edison
Mark Pontti, Champion International Corporation
Bernard Quinlan, ANR Pipeline Company
Dan Robbins, Outdoors Forever
Nancy Sferra, The Nature Conservancy
David Seesholtz and Maya Hamady, Hiawatha National Forest
Tom Smith, Huron-Clinton Metropolitan Authority
Geoff Walsh, Bureau of Land Management, Eastern States
Al Westover and Joe Meszaros, Michigan Department of Transportation

Illustrations by Gijsbert van Frankenhuyzen
Front cover photograph by Carl R. Sams II

Michigan State University Press
East Lansing, Michigan 48823-5202

Contents

Sponsors...5
Preface..7
Wildlife Viewing in Michigan.....................8
Wildlife Viewing Hints............................9
Safety and Ethics..................................11
How to Use This Guide.........................13
Map Information...................................14

Region 1 - Upper Peninsula

Site   Page
1   Isle Royale National Park.......................16
Biodiversity: The Spice of Life.................18
2   Porcupine Mountains State Park.............19
3   Black River Recreation Area....................20
4   Gogebic Ridge Hiking Trail.................21
5   Presque Isle Flowage............................22
6   Clark Lake Day-Use Area.......................23
7   Bat Mine...24
8   Deer Marsh Interpretive Trail.............25
9   Watersmeet Rails to Trails.................25
Weasel Family 26
10 Davidson Lakes 27
11 Bob Lake Campground.....................28
12 Silver Mountain...............................28
13 Keweenaw Peninsula 30
14 Sturgeon River Sloughs....................32
15 Canyon Falls Roadside Park.............33
16 Groveland.......................................33
17 Moose Country...............................34
18 Wetmore Pond.................................35
Carrying Capacity: How Deep is the Barrel?........36
19 Presque Isle Park.............................37
20 Gene's Pond.....................................38
21 Hardwood Impoundment.................38
22 Menominee River/Piers Gorge.............39
23 Peninsula Point................................40
24 Portage Marsh 41
25 Boney Falls Basin.............................41
Songbirds...42
26 Au Train Songbird Trail.....................43
27 Sand Point Marsh Trail/Pictured Rocks
    National Lakeshore..........................44
28 Rainey Wildlife Area.........................45
29 Seney National Wildlife Refuge...........46
30 Big Knob Forest Campground............47
31 Cut River Bridge.............................47
32 Tahquamenon Falls State Park............48
33 Whitefish Point Bird Observatory........49
Succession: Changing Land, Changing Wildlife...50
34 Monocle Lake Trail..........................52

35 Munuscong Wildlife Management Area.........53
36 Horseshoe Bay...................................54
Other Sites in Region 1............................55

Region 2 - Northern Lower Peninsula

Site   Page
37 Ludington State Park...........................57
38 Hamlin Lake Marsh.............................58
39 Lake Bluff Audubon Center.................59
40 North Country Trail.............................60
41 Manistee River...................................61
Hunting, Fishing, and Wildlife Conservation.....62
42 Mitchell State Park Heritage Fisheries
    and Wildlife Nature Study Area.............63
43 Brandybrook Semiprimitive Area............64
44 Sleeping Bear Dunes National Lakeshore.....65
45 Suttons Bay Marsh Boardwalk............66
46 Sand Lakes Quiet Area.......................66
47 Skegmog Swamp Pathway...................67
48 Grass River Natural Area.....................68
49 Jordan River Valley............................69
50 Wilderness State Park..........................70
51 Mill Creek State Historic Park..............71
52 Cheboygan State Park..........................71
What Is a Food Web?..............................72
53 Thompson's Harbor State Park.............73
54 NettieBay Lodge..................................74
55 Tomahawk Creek Flooding.................75
56 Pigeon River Country Elk Range.........76
57 Fletcher Floodwaters..........................77
58 Deward Tract....................................78
59 Hartwick Pines State Park...................79
60 Fletcher Sharptail Area.......................80
61 Dead Stream Flooding.......................81
62 Houghton Lake Flats—South Unit.........82
63 Backus Lake.....................................83
Habitat: Homes for Wildlife 84
64 Marl Lake and South Higgins Lake State
    Park...85
65 Wakeley Lake..................................85
66 Luzerne Boardwalk............................87
Endangered Species: Going, Going, Gone......88
67 Jack Pine Wildlife Viewing Tour........89
68 Au Sable River.................................90
69 Rifle River Recreation Area................91
Waterfowl...92
70 Tuttle Marsh Wildlife Area.................93
71 Tawas Point State Park......................94
72 Wigwam Bay Wildlife Area................95
73 Pinconning County Park....................95
Other Sites in Region 2..........................96

Region 3 - Southern Lower Peninsula

Site		Page
74	Hart-Montague Bicycle Trail State Park	98
75	Haymarsh Lake State Game Area	99
76	Hardy Dam Nature Trail and Muskegon River	100
77	Muskegon State Game Area	101
78	Muskegon State Park	102
79	P.J. Hoffmaster State Park	103
80	Harbor Island	104
The Great Lakes—"Sweet Water Seas"		**106**
81	Kitchel-Lindquist Dunes Preserve	107
82	Blandford Nature Center	108
83	Grand Rapids Fish Ladder	109
84	Pickerel Lake	109
85	De Graaf Nature Center	110
86	Allegan State Game Area	111
87	Kal-Haven Trail	112
88	Sarett Nature Center	113
89	Nipissing Dune Trail	114
90	Berrien Springs Fish Ladder	115
91	Fernwood Nature Center	115
92	West Lake Nature Preserve	116
93	Michigan Fisheries Interpretive Center	117
Birds-of-Prey (Raptors)		**118**
94	Kalamazoo Nature Center	119
95	Yankee Springs State Recreation Area and Barry State Game Area	120
96	Kellogg Bird Sanctuary	121
97	Binder Park Zoo	122
98	Whitehouse Nature Center	123
99	Dahlem Environmental Education Center	124
100	Lost Nation Trail	125
101	Woldumar Nature Center	126
102	Maple River Wetlands	127
What Is a Wetland?		**128**
103	Rose Lake Wildlife Research Area	129
104	Dansville State Game Area	130
105	Haehnle Audubon Sanctuary and Waterloo Recreation Area	131
106	Bird Hills Park	132
107	Pointe Mouillee State Game Area	133
108	Lake Erie Metropark	134
109	Metro Beach Metropark	135
110	Seven Ponds Nature Center	136
111	Lloyd A. Stage Outdoor Education Center	137
112	West Bloomfield Woods Nature Preserve	138
113	Independence Oaks County Park	139
114	Indian Springs Metropark	140
115	Kensington Metropark	141
116	Shiawassee River Wetlands	142
Night Species		**144**
117	Chippewa Nature Center	145
118	Tobico Marsh	146
119	Fish Point State Game Area	147
120	Huron County Nature Center	148
121	Port Crescent State Park	149
Other Sites in Region 3		**150**
Wildlife Index		**151**

This book is dedicated to all those who need to wander forests and fields, smell fresh air and feel wind in their hair, and see firsthand the miracles of the natural world.

-Phil T. Seng and David J. Case

Project Sponsors

Major financial and/or technical support for this project was provided by the following agencies and organizations:

ANR Pipeline Company (ANR), a subsidiary of The Coastal Corporation, operates one of the nation's largest interstate natural gas pipeline systems. ANR provides storage,  transportation and various capacity-related services to a variety of customers in both the United States and Canada. ANR is part of one of the nation's most successful diversified energy firms. ANR's parent firm, the Coastal Corp., is a Houston-based energy holding company with more than $10 billion in consolidated assets and subsidiary operations in natural gas marketing, transmission, and storage; oil and gas exploration and production; petroleum refining and marketing; coal, chemicals, trucking, and independent power production. ANR Pipeline Company, 500 Renaissance Center, Detroit, Michigan 48243, (800) 8-ASK ANR.

The Bureau of Land Management (BLM) is responsible for the management of public lands and resources, balancing resource uses and protection, while maintaining healthy ecosystems. In Michigan, the BLM manages a mineral estate of more than 3.5 million acres and surface acreage of approximately 75,000 acres (surface acres include withdrawals for other agencies). In addition, the BLM is now processing 10 notices of intent to revoke U.S. Coast Guard lighthouse withdrawals at the Coast Guard's request. Eastern States, BLM, 7450 Boston Blvd., Springfield, VA 22153, (703) 440-1668.

Champion International Corporation is a major supplier of business and printing papers, publication papers, newsprint and paperboard products for domestic and international markets. Headquartered in Stamford, Connecticut, the company owns or controls more than five million acres of forestlands in the United States and is also a major manufacturer of plywood and lumber. In Michigan, Champion operates a modern pulp and paper mill in the Upper Peninsula, owns 370,00 acres of forestlands, and employs more than 700 people, earning nearly $38 million annually. Champion International Corporation, P.O. Box 211, Highway U.S. 2, Norway, Michigan 49870, (906) 779-3200.

Consumers Power Company (CPCo) has a historic and continuing commitment in protecting and enhancing the environment while powering Michigan's progress. The many wildlife viewing opportunities on CPCo lands along the Au Sable, Manistee, and Muskegon rivers are the result of careful stewardship dating to the early 1900s. CPCo actively manages corporate lands for wildlife in cooperation with state and federal resource agencies, the Wildlife Habitat Council, Michigan Wildlife Habitat Foundation, The Nature Conservancy, Michigan Nature Association, and many local conservation organizations.

Detroit Edison is Michigan's largest electric utility, serving nearly two million residential, industrial and commercial customers in southeastern Michigan. One of the state's largest property owners, Detroit Edison's 150,000 acres provide habitat for wildlife along shorelines, in undeveloped areas of its power plant sites and along its transmission and distribution corridors. The Company cooperates with a variety of environmental groups including the Michigan Wildlife Habitat Foundation. In addition, the Detroit Edison Foundation supports the work of many nonprofit organizations such as the Wildlife Habitat Enhancement Council, Global ReLeaf of Michigan, the Nature Conservancy and the Greening of Detroit.

The Michigan Department of Natural Resources, Wildlife Division is responsible to properly manage the state's wildlife resources for the use and enjoyment of the public. Financial support for the "Watchable Wildlife" program  is provided by citizen donations through the Division's Nongame Wildlife Fund income tax check-off.

5

The Fund has supported research, education, and construction projects to identify, protect, manage, and restore native plant and animal species, natural communities, and other natural features. In addition, a number of projects have been conducted to promote the public's knowledge, enjoyment, and stewardship of Michigan's natural resources.

The Michigan Travel Bureau is pleased to participate in the Michigan Watchable Wildlife Program and to help sponsor this guidebook, which opens up to the traveling public newly created and signed wildlife sites across the state. This program and guidebook can help generate a new appreciation of Michigan's vast natural resources—along with an awareness of the need to protect wildlife habitat even as we increase the opportunities to observe wildlife in their habitat. The Michigan Travel Bureau welcomes inquiries about nature-based tourism. Just call (800) 5432-YES.

The Michigan United Conservation Clubs (MUCC) is a nonprofit public interest group of individuals and local affiliate groups. MUCC is dedicated to protect Michigan's outdoor heritage; carefully manage its natural resources; promote the conservation of its soils, forest, waters, wildlife and fish; and advocate the right of all citizens to enjoy Michigan's outdoor opportunities. A $25 annual membership in MUCC includes 12 monthly issues of *Michigan Out-of-Doors*® magazine. To join, or for more information, write or call Michigan United Conservation Clubs, P.O. Box 30235, Lansing, Michigan 48909, (517) 371-1041.

The U.S. Fish and Wildlife Service administers 112,448 acres in Michigan. This includes seven national wildlife refuges, three national fish hatcheries, three law enforcement offices, a Great Lakes coordination office, two fisheries biological stations, one fisheries resource office, an ecological services office and a private lands office. The mission of the U.S. Fish and Wildlife Service is to conserve, protect, and enhance fish and wildlife and their habitat for the continuing benefit of the American people. U.S. Fish and Wildlife Service, Henry Whipple Federal Building, 1 Federal Drive, Fort Snelling, MN 55111-4056, (612) 725-3502.

The U.S. Forest Service is responsible for the sound management of National Forest lands and their resources. As stewards for these lands, the Forest Services employs ecosystem management to protect, restore and manage them to best serve the needs of the American people.

> **The Hiawatha National Forest** is located in the central to eastern portion of the Upper Peninsula. It consists of 893,348 acres and is the only national forest adjacent to three of the Great Lakes (Superior, Michigan, and Huron). The Hiawatha offers a variety of unique natural resources that are relatively accessible for its visitors. Hiawatha National Forest, (906) 786-4062.

> **The Huron-Manistee National Forests** in northern lower Michigan are pleased to sponsor this watchable wildlife project. The Huron-Manistee National Forests manage nearly one million acres of public land and have active wildlife, recreation, fisheries, and partnership programs. Huron-Manistee National Forests, 1755 S. Mitchell Street, Cadillac, MI 49601, (800) 821-6263.

Project Contributors

Additional support for this project was provided by the following organizations:

Indiana Michigan Power Company

Michigan Audubon Society

Michigan Department of Transportation

STATE OF MICHIGAN

JOHN ENGLER, Governor

DEPARTMENT OF NATURAL RESOURCES
Stevens T. Mason Building, P.O. Box 30028, Lansing, MI 48909
ROLAND HARMES, Director

Those of us who have spent time in Michigan's great outdoors know we have been blessed by an abundance and diversity of plant and animal species. Each time we hike, camp, bike, fish, or hunt, the presence of wildlife enhances our experience. Michigan is home to wildlife species as large as the 1,800-pound moose, the largest land mammal in North America, down to the karner blue butterfly, an insect with a one-inch wing span. Our state also provides the summer residence of the Kirtland's warbler, one of the rarest birds in the world.

This publication is the culmination of a two-year project involving a partnership of state and federal agencies, private organizations, and industry. We dedicate it to all who share a common interest and dedication to conserving the diversity of Michigan's wildlife heritage and the resources upon which they depend.

The information presented in these pages is intended to provide you with assistance in learning more about our state's natural heritage and where you can go to share in one of the fastest growing outdoor activities: wildlife viewing.

I encourage you to take a little extra time while traveling in Michigan to visit one of the many sites listed in the book and to watch for the brown binoculars signs, which will be erected on roadsides, directing you to designated viewing areas. I hope you and your family will enjoy Michigan's wildlife viewing areas.

Sincerely,

Roland Harmes
Director

PRINTED ON
RECYCLED PAPER

R 1026
9/93

Wildlife Viewing in the Great Lakes State

Michigan has been blessed with a great abundance of wildlife and natural resources and has long been known throughout the country as a destination for outdoor activities such as hunting, fishing, hiking, camping, skiing, and boating. In recent years, wildlife viewing has become a very popular outdoor activity, and again Michigan ranks as one of the premier destinations in the country for pursuing this exciting pastime.

A tremendous variety of wildlife viewing opportunities await you in Michigan's great outdoors.

When French fur traders first arrived in Michigan, towering forests, vast wetlands, and pristine rivers stretched all the way from the shores of Lake Erie to the western Upper Peninsula. Since that time, these resources have spawned and sustained industries that provided jobs and the raw materials used to build America. Although human activities have changed the complexion of the land, Michigan is still a state of natural superlatives, such as:

- Shorelines on 4 of the 5 Great Lakes
- Productive wetlands and protected shallows on Great Lakes bays and inlets
- More freshwater shoreline than any other state
- Miles of cold, clear streams and rivers
- Vast tracts of hardwood and conifer forest
- More than 100 waterfalls in the Upper Peninsula alone
- One of the largest designated wilderness areas east of the Mississippi River

These diverse habitats provide homes for more than 750 kinds of fish, amphibians, reptiles, mammals, and birds—enough to provide a lifetime of viewing opportunities.

This guide features 121 of the best places in Michigan to view wildlife. Certainly there are many more waiting to be explored, but these are great places to start. Some sites in this guide are barrier-free, others are rugged and undeveloped. No matter where you are in the state, there are sites in this guide only minutes away.

This book is not intended to be a guide to state hunting and fishing areas, but these activities are permitted on many of the sites included here. Hunting and fishing symbols appear on the write-up for each site where these activities are permitted. Many people are not aware that money from hunting and fishing licenses and tax money from the sale of hunting and fishing equipment is used to pay for the purchase and management of fish and wildlife habitat in Michigan and throughout America. In Michigan, hunters are responsible for the purchase of nearly one million acres of public land, including many of the sites that appear in this guide.

Getting the Most From Your Trip

Like most recreational activities, wildlife viewing can be as simple or as involved as you want it to be. There are situations where you can be successful without ever leaving your car or back porch swing; on the other hand, there are experiences that require extensive planning, dedication, and physical stamina.

Wildlife viewing is an exciting activity, and much of this excitement stems from the fact that you can never be sure what you might see. If you spend much time at all at any of the sites in this book, you will see wildlife of one kind or another. Some days will be better than others, but there are several things you can do to greatly increase your chances of success.

Binoculars and spotting scopes can bring you "up close and personal" with wildlife without disturbing natural behaviors.

Easy does it
The best way to see more wildlife more often is to slow down. Walk softly and quietly and try to blend into the environment. Stop often to look and listen.

Timing is everything
Different wildlife are active at different times of day, so it helps to know a little about the animals you wish to see. For instance, red-tailed hawks soaring on thermal air currents might best be viewed during the heat of a summer afternoon, while flying squirrels will only be seen by the light of the moon. In general, more kinds of wildlife are active in the early morning and late evening than any other time of day.

Choose the season
Just as with time of day, wildlife activity also varies with season. Some animals will not be found during the cold Michigan winter. Many kinds of birds and a few kinds of insects migrate south; many small mammals hibernate; and reptiles and amphibians burrow under-

Wintertime offers some unique and outstanding wildlife viewing opportunities. Try combining wildlife viewing with cross-country skiing or snowshoeing.

ground and become dormant. On the other hand, winter is often a good time to view white-tailed deer because their brown coats stand out against the snowy ground.

Use equipment to help

There is a tremendous variety of equipment and accessories available to help you get the most out of your wildlife viewing excursions. All of these are optional—you don't have to own any fancy equipment to see wildlife—however, these things can greatly enhance your viewing experiences.

- **Binoculars or spotting scopes** - A pair of binoculars makes a great addition to a wildlife viewing trip. They bring the action right up close where you can see colors and behavior that you would never see with the naked eye.

- **Field identification guides** - The *Michigan Wildlife Viewing Guide* contains some very basic wildlife identification techniques, but they are only the tip of the iceberg. There are numerous pocket-size field guides available that collectively can help you identify nearly every plant and animal in Michigan. These guides also contain specific information about the habits and behaviors of the wildlife you are trying to view.

- **Road map or atlas** - This wildlife viewing guide contains locator maps and written directions to help you find the listed sites. However, a good state or county road map can point out many other interesting sites and attractions nearby that you might otherwise pass by.

- **Carrying case** - A backpack or other carrying case can be very handy for storing all your equipment. Keeping your equipment in one place makes it easy to grab the bag and go wildlife viewing at a moment's notice.

Come prepared

The sites in this guide encompass the full range of outdoor experiences, from indoor viewing windows, to paved trails, to back-country wilderness. Be sure you know what to expect before making your visit. Check the facilities icons listed for each site and prepare accordingly. If you have questions, call the site owner or manager for more information. It is always a good idea to bring boots, rain gear, bug spray, and water. At wilderness or undeveloped sites, be sure to bring maps and a compass, and know how to use them.

All in good time

Patience is a virtue for wildlife watchers. If you jump out of your car at a site expecting to see all of the listed wildlife right away, you probably will be disappointed. Animal movements and behavior patterns often are very unpredictable, which can be a source of frustration—or fascination. The key is to learn where to go and how to look, and then just hang in there!

Just one more trail...

Wildlife watching is a great reason to get out on the ground and hike "just one more trail" or float "just one more river." It offers the challenge of pursuit, the thrill of the unexpected, and the peace of primeval solitude. You never know what lies around that next bend, so why not check it out?

Doing It Right

Many people do not realize that wildlife viewing can be harmful to animals and ecosystems if it is not done properly. Most wildlife watchers are genuinely concerned about the plants and animals they are trying to observe. By following these few, simple guidelines, you can ensure a safe, healthy experience—for yourself and for wildlife.

Keep your distance

The goal of all wildlife watchers should be to observe nature without disturbing or altering it. The most common mistake people make is trying to get too close to wildlife. It's a natural urge, but remember, under certain conditions, a single disturbance may lead to an animal's death. A spooked animal might become injured or killed trying to flee, or it may abandon a nest or quit feeding during a time of critical energy need.

Almost everyone recognizes the striped skunk—by sight *and* by smell!

Let it be

Chasing an animal may lead directly to its death, such as causing it to run onto a highway or jump into a river. Chasing also has an indirect impact too. When an animal is forced to flee, it uses up energy that it needs to survive. Don't stare directly at large animals such as moose, elk, or bears. They may interpret this as a threat, causing unpredictable results. Pets and wildlife do not mix. If given the chance, domestic animals will almost always chase or harass wildlife, and may also spread or receive diseases from wildlife. Pets are best left at home, but if you do bring one along, be sure you keep it on a leash and under control—especially during the spring and summer nesting season.

Though it appears "cute and cuddly," this red fox pup—like all wildlife—would not make a good pet.

You're not my mother

It is fairly common to see young or "baby" animals by themselves during spring. Although they may appear to be orphaned or abandoned, this is rarely the case. Too often, well-meaning people remove young animals from the wild, thinking they are saving them, when in fact the parents of the young were standing by, just out of sight. Even if an animal is an orphan, you should leave it alone. Many animals will defend themselves by scratching or biting. Also, your scent on a young animal may hamper efforts to return it to the wild. Report orphaned animals to the site manager.

Do unto others...

If you arrive at a site that already has other people watching wildlife, be considerate as you approach. Slamming your car doors, talking too loudly, or moving too quickly might frighten the wildlife and ruin the experience for everyone.

Get permission

Private land in Michigan is protected by law and you must have permission from the landowner before you can enter legally. When visiting public lands, be aware of and respect all property boundaries.

Many boardwalk hiking trails in Michigan can take you right into the middle of wetlands, dunes, and other fragile habitats.

Stay on the trails (where appropriate)

At some wildlife viewing sites, visitors are encouraged to hike wherever they please. However, other sites may contain rare plants or fragile ecosystems where access must be limited to protect the resource from trampling, soil compaction, or erosion. Obey all site regulations and report violations to the site manager.

Leave it better than you found it

Few things can spoil the atmosphere of an adventure in the great outdoors faster than the sight of an old soda can or broken bottle. It goes without saying that you should always pack out your trash or dispose of it properly. Many wildlife watchers go one step further by carrying a small trash sack with them and picking up litter that senseless people have left behind. You can also help by reporting littering and vandalism to the site manager.

Don't get bugged

If you spend time outdoors in Michigan during late spring and summer, know that insect pests are going to be part of the experience. Mosquitoes, black flies, deer flies, and ticks can be very abundant. The key is to be prepared so they don't ruin your experience. Sometimes a little bug spray is all you will need; other times you will find long pants, long sleeves, a headnet, and bug spray to be essential. When you return, be sure to check yourself thoroughly for ticks—especially the tiny deer tick which can be a carrier of Lyme's disease.

How To Use This Guide

For easy reference, this guide divides the state into three viewing regions, the Upper Peninsula, the Northern Lower Peninsula, and the Southern Lower Peninsula. There is a separate section of the book for each region. Each section has color bars along the page borders that make it easy to locate the region you wish to see. Region maps at the beginning of each section show the viewing sites, cities and towns, and major roads in the region. Sites are numbered consecutively from 1-121, beginning in the Upper Peninsula and proceeding west to east and north to south within each region.

The following information is provided for each site in this guide:

Site Description: brief description of what the site looks like and some of the physical features you will find there (e.g. dunes, rolling forest, wetland, etc.).

Wildlife Viewing: lists the featured wildlife to be viewed at the site. When appropriate, this section tells the best season and time of day to see the featured wildlife and also may contain interesting facts about wildlife that may be seen at the site.

Directions: includes a map and written description of how to get to the site from the nearest town or major road.

Ownership: lists the name of the agency or organization that owns or manages the site, and gives a telephone number to call for more information.

Size: gives the approximate area of each site, usually in acres. (An acre is about the size of a football field.)

Closest Town: gives the name of the town or village closest to the site.

Facilities Symbols: represent some of the facilities and recreational opportunities available at the site. Contact the site owner/manager for details.

1. Restrooms	6. Cross-country Skiing	11. Fishing
2. Trails	7. Boat Ramp	12. Hunting
3. Picinic	8. Restaurant	13. Entry Fee
4. Camping	9. Lodging	14. Bicycling
5. Visitor Center	10. Drinking Water	15. Barrier Free

In addition to wildlife viewing sites, this guide also contains:

Ecological concepts - interspersed throughout the pages of this guide you will find several one-page descriptions of ecological concepts such as food webs, habitat, and biodiversity. These are quick, interesting explanations of some of the complex interactions that exist among wildlife and the environment.

Wildlife identification pages - five pages of this guide are devoted to wildlife identification. Most wildlife watchers prefer to bring along separate field guides to the birds or other animals they wish to see, but these pages show basic identification techniques for some of Michigan's more popular wildlife.

Other wildlife viewing sites - Michigan is blessed with a bounty of excellent places to view wildlife, and there was not enough room in this book to include them all. However, at the end of each section of this guide, there is a list of other wildlife viewing sites that occur in that region.

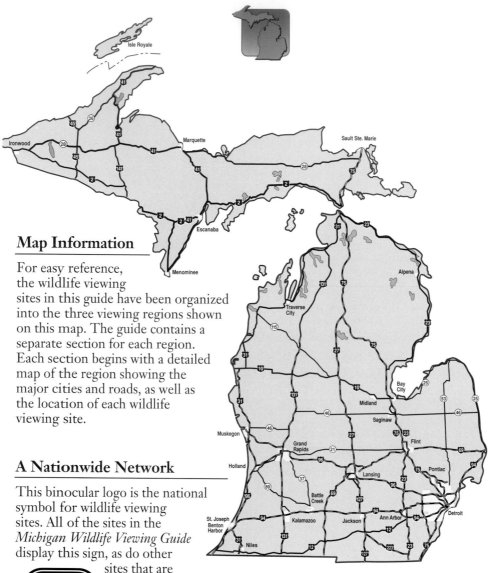

Map Information

For easy reference, the wildlife viewing sites in this guide have been organized into the three viewing regions shown on this map. The guide contains a separate section for each region. Each section begins with a detailed map of the region showing the major cities and roads, as well as the location of each wildlife viewing site.

A Nationwide Network

This binocular logo is the national symbol for wildlife viewing sites. All of the sites in the *Michigan Wildlife Viewing Guide* display this sign, as do other sites that are not included here. You should also watch for this logo on highway signs as you travel outside Michigan, because there is a national network of wildlife viewing sites springing up across the country.

Region 1

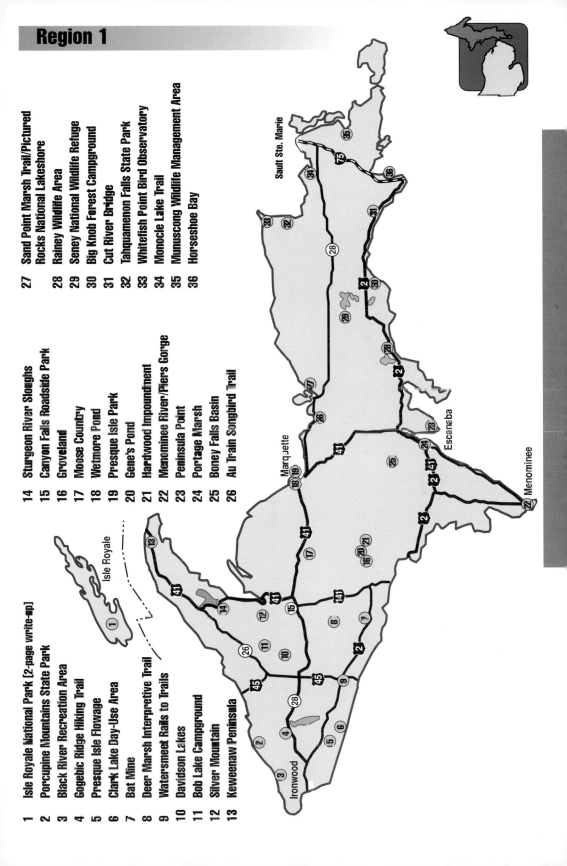

1   Isle Royale National Park [2-page write-up]
2   Porcupine Mountains State Park
3   Black River Recreation Area
4   Gogebic Ridge Hiking Trail
5   Presque Isle Flowage
6   Clark Lake Day-Use Area
7   Bat Mine
8   Deer Marsh Interpretive Trail
9   Watersmeet Rails to Trails
10 Davidson Lakes
11 Bob Lake Campground
12 Silver Mountain
13 Keweenaw Peninsula

14 Sturgeon River Sloughs
15 Canyon Falls Roadside Park
16 Groveland
17 Moose Country
18 Wetmore Pond
19 Presque Isle Park
20 Gene's Pond
21 Hardwood Impoundment
22 Menominee River/Piers Gorge
23 Peninsula Point
24 Portage Marsh
25 Boney Falls Basin
26 Au Train Songbird Trail

27 Sand Point Marsh Trail/Pictured
    Rocks National Lakeshore
28 Rainey Wildlife Area
29 Seney National Wildlife Refuge
30 Big Knob Forest Campground
31 Cut River Bridge
32 Tahquamenon Falls State Park
33 Whitefish Point Bird Observatory
34 Monocle Lake Trail
35 Munuscong Wildlife Management Area
36 Horseshoe Bay

Site Description: Isle Royale is a pristine island wilderness area. Its rocky cliffs and jagged coastline stand in stark contrast to the flat blue surface of Lake Superior. The island is 45 miles long and 9 miles wide and contains more than 160 miles of hiking trails. Wheeled vehicles are not permitted on the island and low-impact camping is required, making this site is a backpacker's dream.

Wildlife Viewing: A visit to this site is a special experience that will remain with you forever. The beauty of this pristine wilderness— trees, wildflowers, water, and wildlife—is difficult to describe. Isle Royale offers visitors a chance to completely immerse themselves in a unique island ecosystem. Whether you tour the island on foot or by boat, wildlife viewing opportunities are abundant.

The howl of the timber wolf is a trademark of the wild North Woods. For centuries humans have feared and misunderstood these intelligent, social animals.

Numerous private ferry and seaplane services are available to transport you and your gear to the island, and the Rock Harbor Lodge is open approximately June through September. Low-impact camping is permitted throughout the island. Isle Royale is not the kind of site where you can "drop in"— just getting there requires a six-hour ferry ride from Houghton. Call ahead for details and reservations.

Set aside by Congress in 1931, this national park was designated part of the National Wilderness Preservation System in 1976 and designated as a Biosphere Reserve by the United Nations in 1981.

For most visitors to Isle Royale, moose and wolves are at the top of their wildlife viewing wish list. Moose are seen fairly commonly, often at very close range. Hike slowly and quietly almost anywhere on the island for an opportunity to see one of these huge members of the deer family. Moose came to Isle Royale in the early 1900s, probably swimming from the Canadian mainland. Because they had no natural predators on the island at that time, the moose population grew rapidly until there was not enough food to go around. With nothing left to eat, the moose population crashed due to starvation. Over time, the plants that had sustained the moose slowly began to grow back. As the few remaining moose found more and more food, they again began to reproduce rapidly, and the cycle started all over again.

In the winter of 1948-49 a pack of eastern timber wolves crossed the ice of Lake Superior to Isle Royale. Wolves are natural predators of moose, but the relationship between these two species is very complex. The interactions among wolves, moose, and the island's vegetation have been the subject of pioneering wildlife research—research that continues today. The stealthy and secretive wolves are rarely seen, but a few lucky wildlife watchers catch glimpses of them occasionally.

In addition to moose, opportunities for viewing common loons, beaver, and red foxes are excellent. Beaver activity may be seen anytime along the hiking trails and streams. The beavers themselves are mostly nocturnal (active at night), but they may be seen during the last light of the day.

Before making the trip to Isle Royale, visitors should do some advance reading on the wildlife and other natural resources of this special place. It will make the trip much more interesting and fulfilling.

Isle Royale offers a peaceful, picturesque, wilderness experience. Visitation is limited to keep it that way. Yellowstone National Park has more visitors in one day than Isle Royale has all year. Most of the people you encounter here—whether on the ferry, on the trail, or in the only restaurant at Rock Harbor—are seeking that same wilderness experience.

Directions: Wheeled vehicles including automobiles, scooters, and bicycles are not permitted on the island. However, you may transport a motorboat or canoe to the island on the National Park Service ferry. Ferry services operate from Houghton, Copper Harbor, and from Grand Portage, Minnesota. Seaplane service is also available in Houghton.

Ownership: National Park Service (906) 482-0984

Size: 210 square miles

Closest Towns: Houghton, Copper Harbor

The sun sets on another beautiful day of wildlife viewing along Isle Royale's shoreline. Wildlife are usually more active at dawn and dusk than any other time of day.

David J. Case

Biodiversity: The Spice of Life

Yellow lady's slipper

In its basic form, biodiversity refers to the variety of native plants, animals, and other living organisms that inhabit the earth. Some people like to think of biodiversity as another word for nature.

Brook trout

The variety of life on earth is incredible. There may be as many as 30 million total species, yet scientists have discovered fewer than 2 million so far. Individual animals within any one of these species may have different sizes, colors, and behaviors. A wide diversity of species share an environment and interact with each other in an ecosystem. Finally, the landscape of each continent on earth is a patchwork quilt of unique ecosystems that run together and overlap. All of these factors contribute to the earth's biodiversity—the variety of life.

Gray tree frog

Karner blue butterfly

Why is Conserving Biodiversity Important?

"The first rule of intelligent tinkering is to save all the parts."* Anyone who has taken something apart and then tried to reassemble it knows this to be true. If a part is lost, the machine will not work very well—if it works at all. And as mechanisms become more complex, the individual parts generally become more and more critical.

River otter

If this is true for machines—if a missing cog or belt can render a car's engine useless—how much more might a missing organism affect the health of an ecosystem whose complexity is overwhelming?

Trumpeter swan

Conservation of the earth's biodiversity must be a primary concern for all people, for when biodiversity is destroyed—at any of its levels—"tune-ups" and "replacement parts" are not available.

Massasauga rattlesnake

*Aldo Leopold, *A Sand County Almanac*, (Oxford University Press, 1966).

Site Description: Stunning scenery, excellent and diverse wildlife viewing opportunities, multiple recreational activities, and a wonderful wilderness experience await all visitors to the "Porkies." More than 90 miles of trails through this pristine wilderness could keep even the most ardent hiker busy for weeks! Other opportunities to explore include skiing (cross-country and downhill), camping, fishing, hunting, cabins, observation towers, spectacular waterfalls, and a visitor center. This 60,000-acre site is one of the few large wilderness areas left in the Midwest.

Wildlife Viewing: There are very few kinds of wildlife native to the Upper Peninsula that cannot be seen at Porcupine Mountains Wilderness State Park. Bald eagles, peregrine falcons, and goshawks all nest on the park. One pair of goshawks nests along the 1-mile interpretive trail at the visitor center. They have been known to "dive-bomb" hikers along the trail! A wildlife observation deck along Beaver Creek Trail provides outstanding viewing of beaver and river otters. Black bears are common in the park, and many have lost some of their natural fear of humans. DO NOT FEED THE BEARS. The park is so vast and the opportunities so diverse that your first stop should be the visitors center to pick up maps, brochures, and other information that will let you get the most out of your visit here.

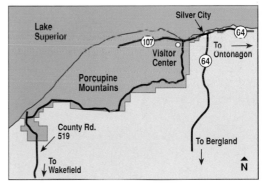

The American black bear is the largest carnivore in Michigan. Although they appear slow and clumsy, black bears are actually quite agile and can sprint short distances at up to 30 miles per hour—nearly as fast as a deer.

Carl R. Sams II

Directions: From Silver City, drive west on M-107 about 3.5 miles to the visitor center.

Ownership: Michigan Department of Natural Resources (906) 885-5275

Size: 60,000 acres

Closest Town: Silver City

Site Description: The scenic Black River corridor is part of the U.S. Forest Service's National Scenic Byway system. Rolling forested hills, stands of old growth timber, river corridor, wetlands, uplands, and waterfalls grace this beautiful site. A campground, group shelter, boat ramp, beach, and other developments can be found in Black River Harbor, while much of the rest of this site is rustic and undeveloped.

Wildlife Viewing: Five picturesque waterfalls along the Black River are major scenic attractions of this site. All are accessible from Black River Road. The North Country National Scenic Trail is another excellent way to access the waterfalls and old growth pine/hemlock forest that line the Black River corridor. When completed, this trail will extend 3,200 miles from New York to North Dakota. For more information contact: North Country Trail Association, P.O. Box 311, White Cloud, MI 49349. Bald eagles have nested along the river near the North Country Trail. In addition to being very scenic, the Black River corridor is home to many uncommon and interesting ferns and wildflowers, and songbird viewing is excellent during spring. Watch for red-eyed vireos, hermit thrushes, pine siskins, and least and great crested flycatchers. Gulls, mergansers, and other waterfowl are common at the campground and day-use area beaches along Lake Superior.

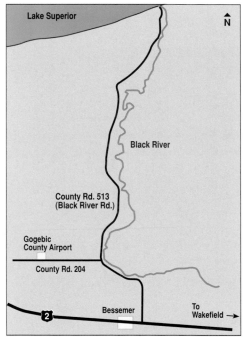

Carl R. Sams II

The beautiful color of the male indigo bunting is caused by the diffraction of sunlight through his feathers. The female is drab brown, helping to conceal her while nesting.

Directions: From Bessemer, drive east on US-2 about 1 mile to County Road 513 (Black River Road). Turn left (north) and follow the signs for the Black River Scenic Byway.

Ownership: U.S. Forest Service (906) 667-0261

Size: 4,500 acres

Closest Town: Bessemer

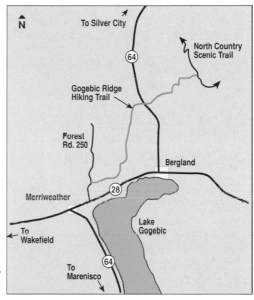

The belted kingfisher is a jay-size bird that is known for its ability to dive head-first into the water after small fish. It also eats crayfish, insects, and mice.

winter wrens, and ovenbirds. Ovenbirds are named for the small nest they build on the forest floor that resembles a dutch oven. Bald eagles and kingfishers are seen occasionally on the banks of Weary Lake.

PORTIONS OF THIS AREA ARE OPEN TO PUBLIC HUNTING. CONTACT THE MICHIGAN DEPARTMENT OF NATURAL RESOURCES FOR AFFECTED SEASONS AND LOCATIONS.

Site Description: Constructed by the Youth Conservation Corps in 1977, this 8-mile linear hiking trail is a great reason to leave the sidewalks and pavement behind. The trail begins by skirting along Weary Lake, then pauses at a rock ledge overlooking Lake Gogebic. Parts of this trail closely follow the Lake Gogebic-Iron River Indian Trail that was used more than 100 years ago. It bends and winds through rolling hills of mixed hardwood and conifer trees before intersecting the North Country National Scenic Trail.

Wildlife Viewing: There is an excellent proba-bility of seeing many kinds of songbirds along the trail, including vireos, thrushes,

Directions: On M-28 in Merriweather, turn north on Forest Road 250 and drive 1.1 miles to a sign marking the trailhead.

Ownership: U.S. Forest Service (906) 884-2411

Size: 7.5 linear miles

Closest Towns: Merriweather, Bergland

Site Description: Located in the bottomlands of the Presque Isle River, this site is an excellent example of the high productivity of wetland habitats. Notice the abundance of plant and animal life found here. Wildlife viewing at this site is probably best done from a canoe or small boat, although limited opportunities do exist from the shore as well.

The crow-size green heron depends on unpolluted wetland areas for survival. It wades in shallow water looking for the fish, crayfish, and frogs that make up most of its diet.

Ted & Jean Reuther

Wildlife Viewing: From April through October, there is an excellent probability of viewing bald eagles throughout this area. A nesting eagle may be viewed by boat in the southwest portion of the Flowage. DO NOT APPROACH OR HARASS NESTING EAGLES! Eagles use the same nest year after year, adding sticks and other new nest material each year. An old eagle nest may weigh several tons!

This site offers good viewing of waterfowl and wading birds like great blue herons from May through October. A silent, stealthy canoeist may even see the secretive American bitterns and black terns that call this site home. The best months to see these birds are June through August.

PORTIONS OF THIS AREA ARE OPEN TO PUBLIC HUNTING. CONTACT THE MICHIGAN DEPARTMENT OF NATURAL RESOURCES FOR AFFECTED SEASONS AND LOCATIONS.

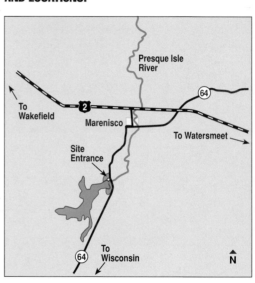

Directions: From Marenisco, drive south on M-64 about 2.5 miles to the site entrance on the right (west) side of the road.

Ownership: U.S. Forest Service (906) 667-0261

Size: 800 acres

Closest Town: Marenisco

Site Description: As part of the 21,000-acre Sylvania Wilderness and Recreation Area, this site has tremendous wildlife viewing potential. The day-use area boasts an 820-acre lake with an extensive natural sand beach and a magnificent stand of virgin northern hardwoods. The 8-mile Clark Lake/Lakeshore Hiking Trail around Clark Lake offers beautiful scenery and excellent wildlife viewing. Visitors must register at the entrance station.

Wildlife Viewing: The stand of large, old trees at this site attracts an interesting and diverse mixture of bird life. Barred owls are common here, and while they are rarely seen during the day, you can often hear their familiar "Who-cooks-for-you, who-cooks-for-you-all" cry at night. The crow-size pileated woodpecker, which has a flaming red crest atop its head, is a common sight as it prospects for insects beneath the bark of old trees. Watch and listen for the many woodland songbirds that live here during summer, including the red-eyed vireo, yellow-rumped and black-throated blue warblers, and oven-bird. There is an excellent probability of viewing loons on Clark Lake. Eagles and osprey may also be seen flying or perching around the lake, and red-tailed hawks nest nearby. Fishers, cat-size members of the weasel family, are seen occasionally during winter. Most of the Clark Lake/Lakeshore Trail lies within the designated wilderness area, so groups of hikers are limited to ten people or fewer. Beautiful wetland areas may be seen along the trail.

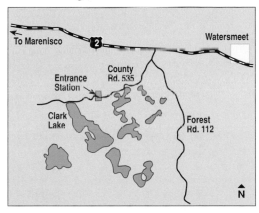

PORTIONS OF THIS AREA ARE OPEN TO PUBLIC HUNTING. CONTACT THE MICHIGAN DEPARTMENT OF NATURAL RESOURCES FOR AFFECTED SEASONS AND LOCATIONS.

Directions: From Watersmeet, travel west on US-2 about 4 miles to County Road 535. Turn left (south) and continue about 4 miles to the entrance to Sylvania Wilderness and Recreation Area.

Ownership: U.S. Forest Service (906) 358-4724

Size: 10 acres

Closest Town: Watersmeet

The red-eyed vireo weaves a suspended nest—an amazing accomplishment for an animal with no hands or fingers!

Like all bats, little brown bats have a sophisticated sonar system that allows them to capture flying insects in total darkness. Bats are very beneficial to humans, consuming thousands of insect pests every night.

Mark Picard

during the day under the bark of trees or in other small crevices. Local businesses cooperated with the Department of Natural Resources to erect a steel cage over the top of the Bat Mine. This structure prevents people from falling into the shaft, but still allows bats to come and go as they please. The best time to view bats is right at dusk, as they begin to emerge from the mine entrance.

Directions: From the intersection of US-141 and US-2, drive west on US-2 for 1.8 miles to Park Avenue (adjacent to a gas station). Turn right (north) and proceed about one mile to the parking area which is just over the hill on the left (west) side of the street. The entrance to the cave is a short walk up the hill from the parking area.

Ownership: City of Iron Mountain (906) 774-8530

Size: 5 acres

Closest Town: Iron Mountain

Site Description:
Site Description: The visible portion of this site is small and inconspicuous—just the mouth of an abandoned iron ore mine that is covered with a special steel grate. But what lies beneath the surface is another story. A steep mine shaft drops about 300 feet into the earth, providing a roosting and hibernation chamber for bats. The mine entrance is just a short walk from the site parking area.

Wildlife Viewing: The Bat Mine is a critical hibernating and breeding location for up to 1 million bats—one of the largest concentrations of bats in the world. Big brown and little brown bats from all over the region come here to hibernate during the cold Michigan winter. Bats begin arriving at the mine in late August and early September. They remain in the mine shaft throughout the winter and begin emerging in late April and May. Some use the mine as their permanent home, but most will disperse during summer to surrounding forest land where they roost

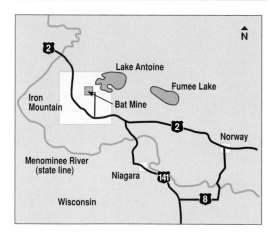

Site Description: The well-maintained interpretive trail at this site gives a close look at the plants and animals that live in and around wetlands. The trail traverses forests and open areas as it snakes around the main body of Deer Marsh.

Wildlife Viewing: Deer Marsh is brimming with a wide variety of wetland wildlife. In the marsh you may see ducks, geese, herons, shorebirds, beavers, and otters. Also watch for deer, eagles, osprey, and songbirds in the uplands and forest surrounding the marsh. The best viewing opportunities occur in the spring, but summer and fall can be good, too.

PORTIONS OF THIS AREA ARE OPEN TO PUBLIC HUNTING. CONTACT THE MICHIGAN DEPARTMENT OF NATURAL RESOURCES FOR AFFECTED SEASONS AND LOCATIONS.

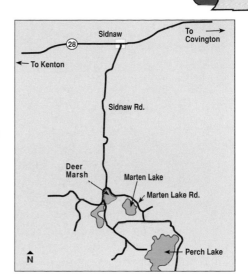

Directions: From M-28 in Sidnaw, drive south on Sidnaw Road about 7.5 miles to Marten Lake Road. Turn left (east) and proceed about 100 feet to the site entrance on the right side of the road.

Ownership: U.S. Forest Service (906) 852-3500

Size: 2.5 linear miles/300 acres

Closest Town: Sidnaw

9   **Watersmeet Rails to Trails**

Site Description: This old railroad grade that has been converted to a linear park runs from the U.S. Forest Service visitor center in Watersmeet to the public library in Land O' Lakes, Wisconsin. The trail cuts cross-country through forests, beaver ponds, clearcuts, and open areas. Bicycles, skis, snowmobiles, ATVs, and pets are all permitted to share this little-used trail with hikers. The trail crosses a stream in which colorful brook trout may be seen along rocks and logs.

Wildlife Viewing: White-tailed deer are common in the forested areas and clearcuts. Beavers, muskrats, mink, and shorebirds may be viewed in and around the floodings created by industrious beavers.

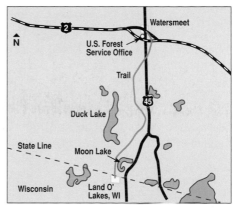

Directions: North trailhead is located at the intersection of US-2 and US-45, 100 yards east of the U.S. Forest Service visitor center parking lot. South trailhead is located at the public library in downtown Land O' Lakes, Wisconsin.

Ownership: U.S. Forest Service (906) 358-4551

Size: 8 linear miles

Closest Town: Watersmeet

Weasel Family

Members of the weasel family vary greatly in size, appearance, and behavior, but they all have low-slung bodies, short legs, and short, rounded ears. Most are nocturnal, so the best time to look for them is at dusk and dawn.

Weasel

Weasels are long and slender. They have brown bodies with white underparts and a black tip on the tail. In winter, they turn completely white except for the tail tip. Adult males are about 12 inches long (including the tail); females are half that size. Weasels spend most of their time on the ground hunting.

Mink

Minks are long and thin, but larger than weasels. Adult males are 20-30 inches long (including the tail). Their bodies are chocolate brown to black except for white chin patches. They live and hunt on the ground near water and are good swimmers.

Marten

Martens are taller and stouter than minks. Adults are about two feet long, including their long, bushy tails. They usually have orange or buff-colored throat patches. Secretive and elusive, martens spend most of their time in the trees.

River otter

The river otter has an elongated body that is very stout and muscular. Adults are 3-4 feet long (including the tail). Otters are chocolate brown on top with lighter brown bellies and silvery chin patches. They are master swimmers and spend nearly all of their time in or near water. Otters are active during the day, but they are very sensitive to human disturbance.

Badger

Badgers have low, wide bodies, short, bowed legs, and long, sharp claws. Adult males are 2-3 feet long; females, somewhat shorter. Their shaggy, coarse fur is mostly grizzled gray, while their legs and snouts are nearly black. The distinctive facial pattern is unmistakable. Badgers live in open fields, farmland, and on woods edges.

Tom Tietz

The large claws and powerful shoulders of the badger make it one of nature's finest diggers. A badger can dig a hole faster than a person with a shovel!

Site Description: This site contains a diversity of habitats and a maze of hiking trails from which to explore them. Pick up a trail brochure at the site (or contact the U.S. Forest Service) and ramble along through mixed pine-hardwood forest, clearcuts, brushy openings, and along wetlands and lakes. There are no facilities here, so come prepared.

Wildlife Viewing: The clearcuts and upland areas of this site are good places to look for deer, ruffed grouse, woodcock, foxes, and black bears. In the open, brushy areas, the lucky observer might catch a glimpse of a coyote or badger. Fishers and martens, Michigan's largest members of the weasel family, are both residents of this site, but these secretive predators are rarely seen by humans. Beavers, river otters, muskrats, and mink call the wetlands of this site home; these aquatic mammals are best seen at dawn and dusk by quiet, stealthy observers. Beavers and muskrats are capable of holding their breath for up to 15 minutes while working or feeding underwater.

PORTIONS OF THIS AREA ARE OPEN TO PUBLIC HUNTING. CONTACT THE MICHIGAN DEPARTMENT OF NATURAL RESOURCES FOR AFFECTED SEASONS AND LOCATIONS.

Directions: From Trout Creek, drive north on Gardner road for five miles to Five Mile Road. Turn right (east) and continue 1 mile. The road turns into a sand trail. Follow it for 3 miles until you see a sign for Davidson Lakes Wildlife Management Area. Park to the left of the sign.

Ownership: U.S. Forest Service (906) 852-3500

Size: 640 acres

Closest Town: Trout Creek

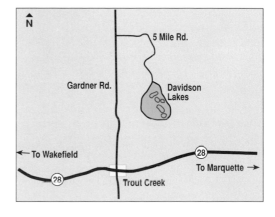

Site Description: A Forest Service campground and the Beaver Lodge Interpretive Trail on this site help visitors explore and experience forest and wetland wildlife. Pick up a trail brochure at the campground trailhead. A portion of this trail is marked with blue diamond markers that designate a short access trail leading to the North Country National Scenic Trail which runs from New York to North Dakota. Contact the Forest Service for more information on the North Country Trail.

Wildlife Viewing: Many kinds of wildlife inhabit this site year-round, but the best months for viewing them are May through July. Watch for beavers, muskrats, and mink in the wetland areas. Lucky viewers might catch a glimpse of the fisher, a large member of the weasel family. Many kinds of waterfowl also live in the wetlands, including mallards, black ducks, wood ducks, and grebes. Sandhill cranes are seen here occasionally.

PORTIONS OF THIS AREA ARE OPEN TO PUBLIC HUNTING. CONTACT THE MICHIGAN DEPARTMENT OF NATURAL RESOURCES FOR AFFECTED SEASONS AND LOCATIONS.

Directions: From Ontonagon, drive east on M-38 to Forest Highway 16. Turn right (south) and continue about 6.5 miles to Pori Road. Turn right (west) and proceed about 2 miles to Forest Road 1470. Turn left (south) and follow the signs to the Bob Lake Campground.

Ownership: U.S. Forest Service (906) 884-2411

Size: 1.25 linear miles

Closest Town: Ontonagon

12   Silver Mountain

Site Description: Beautiful, scenic vistas of the Upper Peninsula await the hearty souls willing to climb the 250-plus boulder-strewn steps to the top of Silver Mountain. The stairs are a rugged climb, and the site offers few amenities, so come prepared.

Wildlife Viewing: In addition to spectacular views of the surrounding countryside, Silver Mountain offers excellent opportunities to view migrating birds-of-prey (raptors). In May-June and again in September-October, watch broad-winged and red-tailed hawks soaring on the strong updrafts of wind that whistle up the mountainside. Smaller sharp-shinned hawks and American kestrels are also common here.

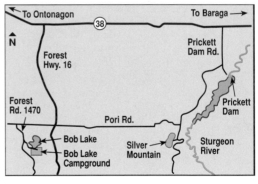

Directions: From Baraga, travel west on M-38 about 9.5 miles to Prickett Dam Road (FS 2270). Turn left (south) and follow the signs to the Silver Mountain parking area.

Ownership: U.S. Forest Service (906) 884-2411

Size: 100 acres

Closest Town: Baraga

Site Description: The Keweenaw Peninsula is the northernmost portion of the Michigan mainland. This long peninsula, famous for its copper industry in the 1800s, reaches almost halfway across Lake Superior toward the Canadian border. There are myriad opportunities for wildlife watchers in the

Sanctuary is one of the few remaining tracts of virgin white pine left in Michigan. For additional information on these sites and other wildlife viewing attractions on the Keweenaw Peninsula, contact the Keweenaw Tourism Council at 1-800-338-7982.

David J. Case

Brockway Mountain Drive offers spectacular views of the surrounding Keweenaw Peninsula.

small area between Eagle Harbor and Copper Harbor; three of the best are Brockway Mountain Drive, Fort Wilkins State Park, and Estivant Pines Nature Sanctuary. Brockway Mountain Drive is the highest American road between the Alleghanies and Rockies. It has numerous pullouts and vistas from which you can look out upon Lake Superior and the surrounding copper country. Fort Wilkins State Park is a long, narrow spit of wooded land that lies between Lake Superior's Copper Harbor and Lake Fanny Hooe. The Lake Superior coastline here is one of the most beautiful stretches of shoreline in the state. Estivant Pines Nature

Wildlife Viewing along Brockway Mountain Drive: This scenic drive offers some of the best scenery in the state. Be sure you bring your camera, especially during fall color season. The biggest wildlife attraction here is the migration of birds-of-prey. From mid-April through mid-June, (mid-May is best), watch hawks, eagles, falcons, and vultures ride the updrafts of air that come across Lake Superior and are forced up the mountainside. Crows, hawks, and ravens also nest on these cliffs. Various facilities are offered along the route and in Eagle Harbor and Copper Harbor.

and Estivant Pines Nature Sanctuary

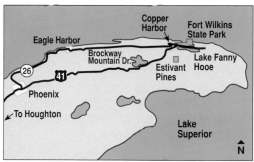

Wildlife Viewing at Fort Wilkins State Park: This park is best known for its 1840s-era wooden fort, but the wildlife viewing opportunities available here are significant as well. Black bears are fairly common in the park and the local area. DO NOT FEED THE BEARS! Red foxes, coyotes, and snowshoe hares live here year-round and may be seen occasionally. Flying squirrels are common residents

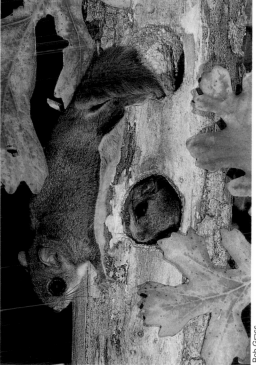

Flying squirrels cannot truly fly, but they are capable of gliding for long distances. When they leap into the air, they stretch their loose folds of skin out tight, forming a miniature "hang glider."

of the park. These small, shy squirrels are often seen at dusk in the large red pines located in the east campground. Although flying squirrels are fairly common throughout Michigan, there are not many locations where they can be easily seen because they are almost strictly nocturnal (active only at night). Watch for them here at dusk as they scamper up trees and launch themselves into gentle glides between trees.

Wildlife Viewing at Estivant Pines Nature Sanctuary: A walk on the trails at this site is like a trip back in time. See a remnant of the 100-foot tall white pines that once covered much of Michigan. Large, colorful, pileated woodpeckers find homes in hollow cavities within the huge pines. The sanctuary also boasts 23 species of ferns and 13 species of wild orchids, so this site is a botanist's dream.

Directions To Brockway Mountain Drive: From Houghton, drive north on US-41 to M-26 at Phoenix. Turn left (northwest) and continue past Eagle Harbor. About 3 miles past Eagle Harbor, follow the signs to Brockway Mountain Drive. The Drive ends at Copper Harbor.

To Fort Wilkins State Park and Estivant Pines: Enter Copper Harbor on US-41/M-26 and follow the signs to Fort Wilkins State Park or Estivant Pines Nature Sanctuary.

Ownership: Michigan Department of Natural Resources (906) 289-4215

Michigan Nature Association

Size: Brockway Mountain Drive: 9.5 linear miles

Fort Wilkins State Park: 203 acres

Estivant Pines Nature Sanctuary: 377 acres

Closest Town: Copper Harbor

Fort Wilkins State Park facilities:

Estivant Pines facilities:

Site Description: Located just off US-41, this site provides a wonderful look at the wetlands associated with the Portage and Sturgeon Rivers. An observation tower adjacent to the parking area gives visitors a panoramic view of this wildlife area. A 1.5 mile nature trail and boardwalk begins at the parking area. Interpretive signs along the trail provide information on the wildlife that visitors may encounter.

Wildlife Viewing: This wildlife area is encircled by dikes that allow wildlife biologists to raise and lower water levels for the benefit of waterfowl, shorebirds, and other wetland wildlife. In addition to the ducks and geese found here, it is common to see great blue herons, bald eagles, and osprey in and around this attractive wetland area. Beavers and muskrats also make their homes here and are best viewed at dawn and dusk.

PORTIONS OF THIS AREA ARE OPEN TO PUBLIC HUNTING. CONTACT THE MICHIGAN DEPARTMENT OF NATURAL RESOURCES FOR AFFECTED SEASONS AND LOCATIONS.

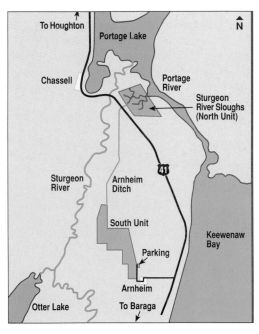

The mink spends most of its time in or near the water in wetland habitats. It is a fierce predator, capable of killing muskrats twice its size.

Jeff Vanuga

Directions: From Chassell, drive south on US-41 about one mile to site entrance on the left side of the road.

Ownership: Michigan Department of Natural Resources (906) 353-6651

Size: 2,800 acres

Closest Town: Chassell

15   Canyon Falls Roadside Park

Site Description: This small park located 14 miles south of Baraga offers a boardwalk through a cedar swamp and a great view of the scenic Canyon Falls of the Sturgeon River. For a closer look at the river, take a cross-country hike or backpack camping trip through the nearby Sturgeon River Gorge Wilderness Area of the Ottawa National Forest. The area is primitive and undeveloped with few trails or access roads. Come prepared for a wilderness experience. The parking lot for this area is not plowed during winter.

Wildlife Viewing: The mature northern hardwood forest along Canyon Falls is a wonderful place to view songbirds. Woodpeckers in particular are attracted to the large, old trees found here. Ruffed grouse may also be seen or heard drumming during spring. The Sturgeon River Gorge Wilderness Area provides stunning views of the Sturgeon River Gorge and surrounding countryside. It is a great place to view fall colors and watch hawks and eagles soaring. White-tailed deer, black bear, ruffed grouse, and snowshoe hares are common in the rolling forested hills of mixed hardwood and conifer trees.

Directions: From the intersection of US-41 and M-28, drive north on US-41 about 3 miles to the Canyon Falls Roadside Park on the left side of the road.

Ownership: Michigan Department of Transportation (906) 524-6124
U.S. Forest Service (906) 852-3500
Michigan Technological University (906) 524-6181

Size: 10 acres

Closest Town: Alberta

16   Groveland

Site Description: The Groveland Iron Ore Mine stopped production in 1980. Settling basins at the abandoned mine now provide habitat for a variety of wildlife and fish species. The unimproved roads leading to this site are rough, especially during spring rains. This road is not recommended for large RVs.

Wildlife Viewing: The water and wetland areas at this site attract wading birds, especially during spring and fall migrations. This site also plays host to bald eagles, loons, ospreys, and cormorants. White-tailed deer are common throughout the year. The old settling ponds now are managed for a variety of game and pan fish, including walleye, bass, perch, and crappie.

PORTIONS OF THIS AREA ARE OPEN TO PUBLIC HUNTING. CONTACT THE MICHIGAN DEPARTMENT OF NATURAL RESOURCES FOR AFFECTED SEASONS AND LOCATIONS.

THE ABANDONED MINE TO THE NORTH OF THE WILDLIFE AREA IS NOT OPEN TO THE PUBLIC AND IS DANGEROUS—DO NOT ENTER.

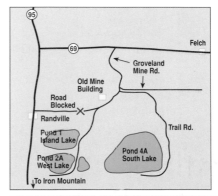

Directions: From the junction of M-69 and M-95 go east on M-69 approximately 3.7 miles to Groveland Mine Road. Drive south on Groveland Mine Road approximately 1.7 miles and then southwesterly into the area.

Ownership: Michigan Department of Natural Resources (906) 875-6622

Size: 5,000 acres

Closest Town: Iron Mountain

The moose is the largest member of the deer family—adult males may stand seven feet tall at the shoulder and weigh 3/4 ton.

Site Description: Many people do not realize that part of Michigan's western Upper Peninsula is home to a free-ranging moose herd. Although it is difficult to predict where moose might be seen on any given day, visitors would do well to begin their quest at Van Riper State Park—near the center of Michigan's moose country. Stop here to get a copy of the *Moose Locator Guide*, which identifies several auto tour routes including the Huron Bay Grade and Tracy Creek Road. Some of the tours listed in the guide are on seasonal roads that may be rugged.

Wildlife Viewing: In 1985 and 1987, 59 moose were released just six miles north of Van Riper State Park and this small herd has been growing ever since. A slow drive along the listed routes or through the area north of the park may result in a sighting of one of these majestic North Woods creatures. Stop at the information center in the park to see a video on moose reintroduction and to get more information on the local herd. In addition to the moose, black bears, deer, coyotes, and foxes may be seen in this area. Hiking

trails ramble throughout the park, connecting several scenic overlooks. Nearby Craig Lake State Park offers additional hiking trails.

Directions to Van Riper State Park: From Champion, drive west on US-41/M-28 about one mile to the park entrance on the left (south) side of the road.

To Huron Bay Grade: From Van Riper State Park, drive west on US-41 about one mile to County Road 607 (Huron Bay Grade). Turn right (north) and travel 3.5 miles to Dishno Creek Road. Turn right (east) and continue about 2 miles to a fork in the road. Bear left and proceed about 10 miles northeast toward Dishno Lake. Return along the same route.

To Tracy Creek Road: From Van Riper State Park, drive west on US-41 to Tracy Creek Road. Turn left (south) and proceed about 16 miles. Drive ends at US-141, about 7 miles south of Covington.

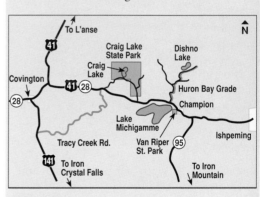

Ownership: Michigan Department of Natural Resources (906) 339-4461

Size: Van Riper State Park - 4,000 acres
Huron Bay Grade - 15 linear miles
Tracy Creek Road - 16 linear miles

Closest Town: Champion

David J. Case

The hiking trail at Wetmore Pond offers scenic views of unique bog habitat.

Site Description: At this site you can hike an undeveloped trail through old-growth forest and around rugged rock outcroppings to a pristine bog habitat at Wetmore Pond. The pond is located on 480 acres of Mead Paper Company land which borders a 2,500-acre tract of the Escanaba River State Forest. The trail is rough and uneven, but the viewing opportunities from the wooden bog observation platform are well worth the effort.

Wildlife Viewing: A bog is a unique wetland habitat that receives very little influx of fresh water. Decaying vegetation causes the water to become acidic, which supports a fragile community of specially adapted plants and animals. Sphagnum moss grows in thick, floating mats on the water's surface and is often mistaken for solid ground. Carnivorous (meat eating) pitcher plants are also common in this habitat. They digest insects to supplement the scarce nutrients available in this acidic environment. During the spring and fall migrations, ducks and geese congregate on the bog, providing excellent viewing opportunities.

PORTIONS OF THIS AREA ARE OPEN TO PUBLIC HUNTING. CONTACT THE MICHIGAN DEPARTMENT OF NATURAL RESOURCES FOR AFFECTED SEASONS AND LOCATIONS.

Directions: From US-41 in Marquette, take Fourth Street north to Wright Street. Turn left (west) and proceed to County Road 550. Turn right (north) and continue about 5 miles to the parking area on the left (west) side of the road.

Ownership: Mead Paper Company (906) 786-1660, extension 2194

Size: 480 acres

Closest Town: Marquette

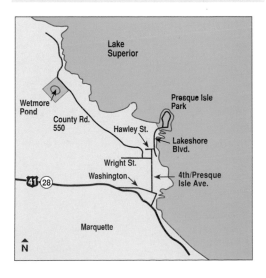

Carrying Capacity: How Deep is the Barrel?

The number of animals a given area of land or water can support over time is called that area's carrying capacity. Consider this illustration representing muskrats in a marsh. The barrel represents the marsh habitat—the amount of food, water, and cover for a fixed number of muskrats. The water in the barrel is the number of muskrats the habitat can support. The pipe pouring water into the barrel represents the new muskrats that are born in the marsh or wander in from other places. The water spilling out is the number of muskrats that die each year due to starvation, predators, disease, or other factors. The barrel can only hold so much water. That is, there is a limit to the number of muskrats that can survive here from year to year unless the habitat (the size of the barrel) is changed in some way. Every parcel of land has a different carrying capacity for every different kind of wildlife that lives there. A pristine cattail marsh would be a deep barrel for muskrats, while a dune forest would hold few, if any.

Who cares how deep the barrel is?

Knowledge of carrying capacity is essential for the conservation and management of wildlife populations. For example, the wolverine requires huge tracts of wilderness to survive—the equivalent of a swimming pool in this illustration. The muskrat, on the other hand, finds everything it needs in a small marsh—a rain barrel by comparison. Biologists use the concept of carrying capacity to determine how much habitat must be conserved to maintain healthy wildlife populations.

Site Description: This small peninsula that juts out into Lake Superior offers scenic vistas and good wildlife viewing just minutes from downtown Marquette. The park's jagged shoreline contains some of the oldest exposed rock formations in North America. A loop trail encircles the peninsula and provides easy-to-moderate hiking and skiing. Camping is not permitted on this site, but there are campgrounds within two miles of the park.

Directions: In Marquette, drive north on Fourth Street (changes into Presque Isle Ave.) to Hawley Street. Turn right (east) and continue to Lakeshore Boulevard. Turn left (north) and follow Lakeshore until it ends at the park entrance.

Ownership: City of Marquette (906) 228-0460

Size: 320 acres

Closest Town: Marquette

Muskrats are common residents of Michigan wetlands. They cut aquatic plants and use them to build dens or "houses" that look like piles of cattail stalks in shallow water areas.

Tom Tietz

Wildlife Viewing: The resident white-tailed deer herd contains several albinos. An albino animal has no pigment in its skin or hide—it appears completely white. Albinism is a genetic trait that is rarely seen in the wild. One reason for its scarcity is that animals lacking protective coloration are very susceptible to predators and rarely have the opportunity to pass their unique lack of color on to the next generation. Muskrats, beavers, turtles, and many kinds of waterfowl are commonly seen along the Lake Superior shoreline. Take the Bog Walk Trail for an up-close look at a 10,000-year-old bog and the specially adapted plants that inhabit this unique type of wetland.

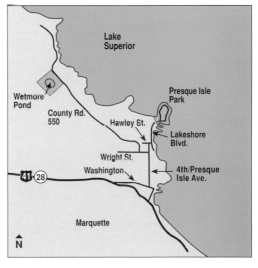

Site Description: This flooding provides excellent habitat for waterfowl, shorebirds, and many other wetland-related wildlife. The site features a nice forest campground, but the best wildlife viewing opportunities are found by canoe or small boat on the impoundment itself.

Wildlife Viewing: This site is a jewel for people who like to view large, unique birds. On the water's surface, watch for loons and cormorants diving for fish. In the treetops near the campground, you can see a great blue heron rookery, or nesting colony. Herons and cormorants both raise their young in this rookery. Boats make good wildlife viewing blinds. There are no motor restrictions on boats in this area, but remember that loud noise or disturbance can cause birds to abandon their nests. High above the water, watch for circling bald eagles and osprey. These aerial hunters will circle above or sit in trees on the shoreline scouting for fish near the surface. Then they fly down low over the surface, snatching fish from the water with their powerful talons.

Directions: From Felch, drive west on M-69 about 1/2 mile to County Road 581. Turn right (north) and proceed about 5 miles to the "Public Access" sign. Turn left (west) and go about one mile to the parking area. Or, drive one mile farther north on County Road 581. From 581, turn left (west) on Leeman Road (County Road 422) and follow the signs to Gene's Pond Forest Campground.

Ownership: Michigan Department of Natural Resources (906) 875-6622

Size: 800 acres

Closest Town: Felch

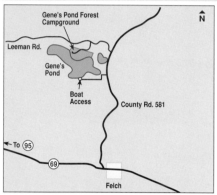

21   Hardwood Impoundment

Description: This area offers some great viewing opportunities of wildlife that have grown accustomed to vehicles passing them along the two dikes that cross the impoundment. A small boat access site is also available.

Wildlife Viewing: Bald eagles nest in the vicinity and are frequently seen roosting or hunting along the dikes. On the lake and wetland areas you may see mallards, Canada geese, grebes, and other waterfowl. Wood ducks are common here and you can see nestboxes that have been erected for them. Along the shoreline look for herons wading in the shallow water. Belted kingfishers are also common in this area. These blue-jay-size birds can be seen plunging headfirst into the water to catch small fish. In the fringe areas around the impoundment, you may see deer, raccoons, and wild turkeys.

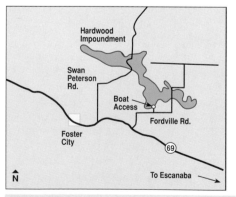

Ownership: Michigan Department of Natural Resources (906) 875-6622

Size: 1,500 acres

Closest Town: Foster City

Site Description: The 40-mile stretch of the Menominee River from above Iron Mountain to Menominee provides a beautiful setting for wildlife watching. Numerous campgrounds and boat access points along the river cater to wildlife watchers with canoes. There are nine hydroelectric power dams and reservoirs on the river, and each has a portage for small boats. The scenic Piers Gorge area of the river contains some of the fastest-moving water in Michigan. It is not navigable, but still offers beautiful scenery and good wildlife viewing from shore.

Wildlife Viewing: This beautiful Menominee River offers spectacular bald eagle viewing opportunities. Eagles are commonly seen all along the river, roosting in tall trees, fishing in the shallow water, or soaring high overhead. This stretch of river also boasts several eagle nests in tall trees right along the shoreline. DO NOT DISTURB OR HARASS NESTING EAGLES. In addition to the eagles, osprey, common loons, and waterfowl are common sightings on this exciting float. Piers Gorge is a very scenic, fast-moving stretch of the river near Florence. The gorge is not navigable, but shoreline trails offer good viewing opportunities for eagles, osprey, and waterfowl. Wisconsin Electric Power Company and Champion International own the Piers Gorge shoreline, and they encourage public use.

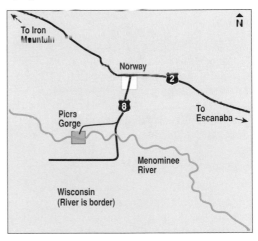

Michigan is known throughout the country for its cool, clear waters. The Piers Gorge area of the Menominee River is a beautiful example.

Tom Parker

THE RIVER CURRENTS AT PIERS GORGE ARE VERY STRONG. DO NOT WADE OR SWIM. KEEP SMALL CHILDREN AND PETS AWAY FROM THE WATER.

Directions: From Norway, drive south on US-8 about 2 miles and follow the signs to Piers Gorge. The road ends at a parking lot at the gorge.

Ownership: Wisconsin Electric Power Company (906) 779-2546

Champion International (906) 779-3271

Size: 60 river miles

Closest Towns: Crystal Falls, Iron Mountain, Menominee, Norway

The great blue heron is easily identified in flight by the way it folds its neck in an S-shape. Herons are most often seen wading in shallow water, hunting for small fish, crayfish, and frogs.

PORTIONS OF THIS AREA ARE OPEN TO PUBLIC HUNTING. CONTACT THE MICHIGAN DEPARTMENT OF NATURAL RESOURCES FOR AFFECTED SEASONS AND LOCATIONS.

Directions: From Rapid River, drive east on US-2 for about 3 miles to County Road 513. Turn right (south) and continue about 18 miles to Peninsula Point. THE FINAL MILE OF ROAD IS VERY ROUGH AND NOT RECOMMENDED FOR RVs OR LONG TRAILERS.

Ownership: U.S. Forest Service (906) 474-6442

Size: 1 acre

Closest Town: Rapid River

Site Description: This site is at the very tip of a long peninsula that sticks out into Lake Michigan. A National Historic Lighthouse sits on the point, and its 40-foot tower makes an ideal vantage point for viewing wildlife and spectacular scenery along the rocky shoreline. A hiking trail through the wooded shoreline offers more "down to earth" wildlife viewing.

Wildlife Viewing: The historic lighthouse on this site makes a great viewing platform. Take a camera and a pair of binoculars up the iron staircase to get a bird's-eye view of ducks, geese, gulls, and shorebirds. During fall and spring migration, this site serves as a natural "launch pad" and "landing strip" for birds that need to rest and feed before or after their long, non-stop flight across Green Bay. Spring warbler viewing is particularly good. Monarch butterflies migrate as well. Thousands of these globe-trotting insects congregate on the Point in the fall before continuing their southward migration to Mexico. Several-to-many great blue herons are usually seen along the shoreline from spring through fall. Heron chicks in a nearby nesting area, or rookery, need a constant food supply to survive and grow. The adults often stalk frogs and small fish in the waters off the Point.

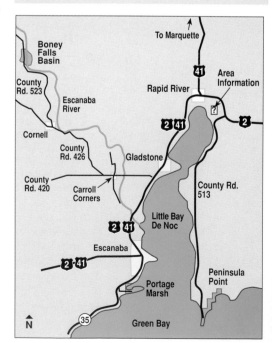

24 Portage Marsh

Site Description: This long, narrow peninsula juts out into the Green Bay portion of Lake Michigan near downtown Escanaba. A cattail marsh between the peninsula and the mainland provides good protective cover for many kinds of wetland wildlife, and there is an unimproved hiking trail that runs along the peninsula. A parking lot and boat ramp give access to the marsh for people who prefer to do their wildlife viewing from boats.

Wildlife Viewing: The wetland area along Portage Point provides a protected oasis for waterfowl during the spring and fall migrations and for some summer resident birds. April and October are generally the best months for viewing migrating waterfowl. A sand beach along one side of the point provides shorebird viewing opportunities. The shorebird migration is not as predictable as the waterfowl migration, but at times it is excellent.

PORTIONS OF THIS AREA ARE OPEN TO PUBLIC HUNTING. CONTACT THE MICHIGAN DEPARTMENT OF NATURAL RESOURCES FOR AFFECTED SEASONS AND LOCATIONS.

Directions: From Escanaba, take M-35 south to Portage Point Road. Turn left (east) and drive to the end of the point.

Ownership: Michigan Department of Natural Resources (906) 786-2351

Size: 200 acres

Closest Town: Escanaba

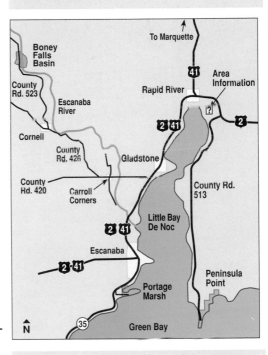

25 Boney Falls Basin

Site Description: This scenic, forested impoundment on the Escanaba River offers beautiful scenery and good wildlife viewing. Hiking trails, small boat access, and a primitive campground add to the attractiveness of this site.

Wildlife Viewing: Eagles and hawks are commonly seen soaring above the impoundment and river corridor. Woodland songbirds are vocal residents in the site's forested areas. The gentle current of the Escanaba River allows canoeists to enjoy a long stretch of river upstream from Boney Falls. Fly fishing for brown trout is popular in this area from June throughout the summer.

THE RIVER IS SHALLOW, SO CANOEING MAY BE DIFFICULT DURING PERIODS OF LOW WATER.

Directions: From US-2/41 south of Gladstone, drive west on South Hill Road, which becomes County Road 426. Follow CR 426 about 11 miles to County Road 523. Continue for 7 miles and turn right (east) at the sign near the dam. The campground and boat access are 1 mile farther north on the right side of the road.

Ownership: Mead Paper, Central District (906) 786-1660

Wells Township, Marquette County

Size: 720 acres

Closest Town: Gladstone

Songbirds

Thrushes

Robins and other thrushes are medium-sized birds that have straight bills. Many are brown with spots or speckles on the breast, and most feed on the ground.

American robin

Yellow warbler

Warblers

Warblers are small birds with slender bills. Most are brightly colored and many have white tail spots and bars on their wings. Usually seen in woods and brushy areas, these birds are very active, rarely sitting still for long.

Sparrows

Sparrows have small bodies and heavy; conical bills which they use to crack open seeds and nuts. Most sparrows are various shades of brown, a few are red, yellow, or blue in color.

Song sparrow

Downy woodpecker

Woodpeckers

Woodpeckers are recognized by their strong, pointed bills and their habit of perching upright on the sides of trees, using their tails as "kickstands." They are most common in forests with many large, old trees.

Gijsbert van Frankenhuyzen

The black-billed cuckoo is an elusive bird of moist thickets and overgrown orchards and pastures. Cuckoos are very beneficial to humans because they eat huge quantities of destructive tent caterpillars and gypsy moth larvae.

Directions: From M-28 in Au Train, turn south onto County Road H-03 (Forest Lake Road/Forest Road 2278) and drive about 4.5 miles to Forest Road 2276. Turn left (east) and continue about 1/2 mile to the campground access on the left side of the road. Take the first campground loop to the right and follow it to the trailhead near campsite #11.

Site Description: The interpretive trail on this site allows visitors to interact with songbirds in their natural habitat. By renting a cassette player and tape in one of several stores in Au Train (A&L Grocery and Au Train Grocery), visitors can learn about and possibly communicate with 20 species of birds common to the area. The trail passes through uplands and forest, along a stream corridor and a bog, and provides access to an observation platform that surveys a shallow bay of Au Train Lake and its surrounding wetlands.

Wildlife Viewing: The Au Train Campground and Songbird Trail are excellent areas for spring birding. In May and June, it is possible to view more than a dozen species of warblers, including the magnolia, black and white, Connecticut, Nashville, Wilson's and Bay-breasted warblers. From the observation platform, watch for bald eagles, ospreys, waterfowl, and many different kinds of shorebirds, including killdeer, greater yellowlegs, American bittern, and spotted, least, and solitary sandpipers.

PORTIONS OF THIS AREA ARE OPEN TO PUBLIC HUNTING. CONTACT THE MICHIGAN DEPARTMENT OF NATURAL RESOURCES FOR AFFECTED SEASONS AND LOCATIONS.

Ownership: U.S. Forest Service (906) 387-2512

Size: 3 linear miles

Closest Town: Au Train

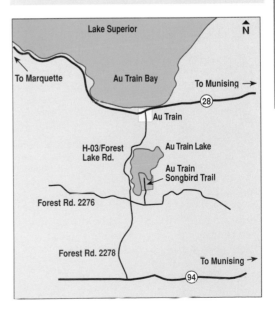

Site Description: The Sand Point Marsh Trail is a 1/2-mile barrier-free boardwalk that provides visitors access through a scenic wetland area at Pictured Rocks National Lakeshore. This trail is merely the tip of the iceberg of the tremendous natural resources to be enjoyed at this large, beautiful National Park service area. The park encompasses the jagged sandstone cliffs, sand dunes, and upland forest of Lake Superior's shoreline from Munising to Grand Marais.

Wildlife Viewing: Beavers are very active in the wetland of the Sand Point Marsh Trail. These aquatic mammals are mostly active at night, but you may see them at dawn and dusk, and evidence of their presence is all around. Waterfowl, herons, and wetland-

PLEASE STAY ON MARKED TRAILS AND DO NOT DISTURB THE NATIVE PLANTS AND WILDLIFE.

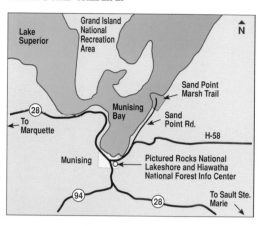

These visitors to Pictured Rocks National Lakeshore are using binoculars to get a close look at wildlife without disturbing the environment or altering wildlife behavior.

David J. Case

Directions: The visitor center is located at the intersection of M-28 and H-58 in the center of Munising. To get to the Sand Point Marsh Trail, follow H-58 north from the visitor center to Washington Street. Turn north on Washington and proceed past the hospital, where the street name changes to Sand Point Road. Continue for 2 miles on Sand Point Road to the parking area.

related songbirds all may be seen in and around this marsh area. Sixteen interpretive exhibits relate the natural and cultural history of the trail. Be sure to stop at the visitor center in Munising to pick up trail maps, interpretive brochures, and additional information about the tremendous wildlife watching opportunities available throughout the park. A large-print trail guide is available for visually impaired visitors.

Ownership: National Park Service (906) 387-3700

Size: Trail area is 25 acres

Closest Town: Munising

Site Description:
Hiking trails, boardwalks, and an elevated observation platform provide outstanding views of wildlife in and along Smith Creek, Smith's Slough, and Indian Lake. This site has no facilities, so come prepared.

Wildlife Viewing:
Songbirds are plentiful along the trails and boardwalks adjacent to the parking area. The spring and fall warbler migrations are especially good. Walk slowly and quietly along the trails for best results. Sometimes you can call warblers into view by standing very still and making a soft "pssh pssh pssh" sound. There is a moderate to high probability of viewing bald eagles and ospreys from the observation platform in spring, summer, and fall. The platform is also a great place to view and photograph the fall colors.

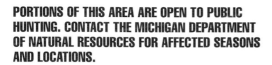

The bright color of the yellow warbler signals the end of winter in Michigan. Yellow warblers often nest in brushy trees along streams and wetland areas.

PORTIONS OF THIS AREA ARE OPEN TO PUBLIC HUNTING. CONTACT THE MICHIGAN DEPARTMENT OF NATURAL RESOURCES FOR AFFECTED SEASONS AND LOCATIONS.

Directions: From US-2 in Manistique, drive north through town on M-94 about 5 miles to Dawson Road. Turn left (west) and proceed 1.5 miles to an access road that goes north to the site parking lot.

Ownership: Michigan Department of Natural Resources (906) 293-5131

Size: 100 acres

Closest Town: Manistique

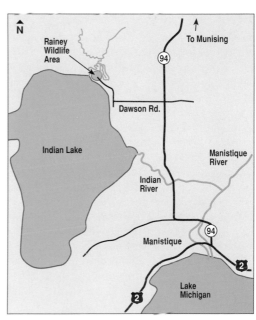

Site Description: One of the premier wildlife viewing sites in the state, Seney National Wildlife Refuge has something to offer wildlife watchers of all types. The refuge encompasses 7,000 acres of managed wetlands, a 9,500-acre bog, and 25,000 acres of wilderness. There are hiking trails, a self-guided auto tour, 70 miles of biking trails, a canoeable river, ski trails, hunting, fishing, and an excellent visitor center. The visitor center is open 9 a.m. to 5 p.m. 7 days a week from May 15 to October 15. Stop in to pick up some of the many maps, brochures, and interpretive materials that will help you get the most out of your visit to this wildlife viewing haven.

PORTIONS OF THIS AREA ARE OPEN TO PUBLIC HUNTING. CONTACT THE REFUGE STAFF OR THE MICHIGAN DEPARTMENT OF NATURAL RESOURCES FOR AFFECTED SEASONS AND LOCATIONS.

Wooden observation platforms give visitors "ringside seats" to wildlife viewing opportunities at Seney National Wildlife Refuge.

Wildlife Viewing: Seney's list of commonly seen critters reads like a wildlife watcher's wish list. There are excellent opportunities to view bald eagles, common loons, trumpeter swans, ospreys, sandhill cranes, and white-tailed deer. Some lucky visitors also catch glimpses of black bears, bobcats, river otters, and moose. Wolves are found at this site, but sightings are very rare. All told, Seney is home to more than 200 kinds of birds, 45 mammals, and 26 fish. The 7-mile Marshland Wildlife Drive is a must for wildlife viewers visiting the refuge (open May 15-October 15). The road is constructed on the tops of water control dikes, so wetland wildlife can be seen at close range on both sides of the road. The drive has three observation decks for viewing wildlife. Stop at the visitor center to get a map of the drive. A 1.5-mile hiking trail that begins at the visitor center also provides viewing opportunities. Volunteers and U.S. Fish and Wildlife Service staff at the visitor center can direct you to the best places to see specific kinds of wildlife.

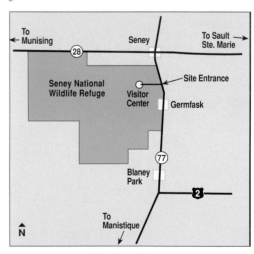

Directions: From Seney, drive south on M-77 for 5 miles to the site entrance on the right (west) side of the road.

Ownership: U.S. Fish and Wildlife Service (906) 586-9851

Size: 95,000 acres

Closest Towns: Seney, Germfask

30 Big Knob Forest Campground

Site Description: This site features some beautiful dune and swale habitat on the shores of Lake Michigan. Wind and water from the lake are constantly sculpting and changing this sandy habitat. Visitors may stay at the forest campground or come for a day hike on the Big Knob-Crow Lake Foot Trails.

Wildlife Viewing: There is a high probability of viewing ducks, geese, and gulls along the beach and the small ponds behind the first dune. Common loons and bald eagles may also be seen here from spring through fall. A stand of northern pin oak trees (unique for this area) may be seen along the road about 1/2 mile before the campground entrance. The sand dune habitat of this site is home to many rare and unique plant species, including the Huron tansy, Houghton's goldenrod, pitcher thistle, and dwarf lake iris. Please do not pick or disturb any of the plants that have managed to establish themselves in this fragile dune environment.

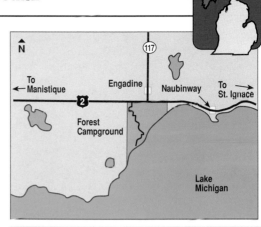

Directions: From Naubinway, drive west on US-2 about 7.5 miles to signs for Big Knob Forest Campground on the left (south) side of the road. After turning left, the Big Knob-Crow Lake Foot Trail is 4.5 miles and the campground is 6 miles down the road.

Ownership: Michigan Department of Natural Resources (906) 293-5131

Size: 6,400 acres

Closest Town: Engadine

31 Cut River Bridge

Site Description: A Michigan Department of Transportation roadside park is the primary access to a network of hiking trails that wind in and around the beautiful Cut River Valley along Lake Michigan.

Wildlife Viewing: Although a rest stop or picnic at the State Roadside Park provides a beautiful view of Lake Michigan and the mouth of the Cut River Gorge, the real beauty of this site lies hidden among the rolling, forested dunes of the Lake Superior State Forest. Hike these trails in May to view spring wildflowers such as trout lily, trilliums, and Dutchman's breeches. Spring is also a good time to view migrating warblers and other songbirds. The trails at this site are equipped with markers to help visitors identify plants and trees along the way.

PORTIONS OF THIS AREA ARE OPEN TO PUBLIC HUNTING. CONTACT THE MICHIGAN DEPARTMENT OF NATURAL RESOURCES FOR AFFECTED SEASONS AND LOCATIONS.

Directions: From Epoufette, travel east on US-2 about 2 miles to the Cut River Bridge State Roadside Park on the left (north) side of the road.

Ownership: Michigan Department of Natural Resources (906) 293-5131

Size: 400 acres

Closest Town: Epoufette

Site Description: Tahquamenon Falls is the second largest state park in Michigan, covering more than 38,000 acres. Most of the park is undeveloped with little vehicular access. The North Country Hiking Trail traverses the park and provides a look at the wilderness interior of this scenic site. Two natural waterfalls on the Tahquamenon River give this park its name. The Upper Falls is one of largest waterfalls east of the Mississippi River and may be the best-known attraction in the Upper Peninsula. The park has four campgrounds to accomodate visitors.

The Upper Falls of the Tahquamenon River is one of the premier scenic attractions in Michigan; but don't forget to look beyond the falls to the excellent wildlife viewing opportunities that await throughout the park.

community, groves of virgin northern hemlock, and miles of scenic river. While hiking the trail, watch

Wildlife Viewing: This entire park provides unique and wonderful wildlife viewing opportunities. The Betsy Lake area offers 3 pristine lakes that make a beautiful canoe float. Contact the park office for access information. The park is home to several notable bird species including the gray jay, boreal chickadee, and Connecticut warbler. The park also contains the state's best breeding site for the palm warbler and one of the only known breeding sites for the rusty blackbird. The area between the upper and lower falls is accessible only by a rustic hiking trail, and features an old-growth American beech/sugar maple

and listen for species associated with this unique combination of habitats. The black-throated green warbler, osprey, river otter, and several species of ferns and wild orchids are just a few examples. The area around the mouth of the Tahquamenon River also offers a variety of interesting plants and animals. Loons and other waterfowl are numerous here, especially during spring migration. Moose are seen occasionally and river otters have a den nearby.

DEER FLIES, BLACK FLIES, AND MOSQUITOES CAN BE VERY NUMEROUS FROM MAY THROUGH JULY, SO COME PREPARED.

Directions: East Entrance: From Paradise, drive south on M-123 about 5 miles to the park entrance on the right (west) side of the road. West Entrance: From Paradise, drive west on M-123 about 6 miles to the park entrance on the left (south) side of the road.

Ownership: Michigan Department of Natural Resources (906) 492-3415

Size: 38,000 acres

Closest Town: Paradise

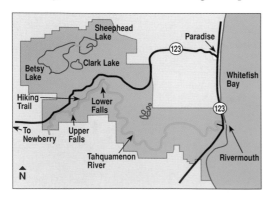

Phil Burkhouse

The great gray owl is a huge and elusive bird found mostly in Canada. They occasionally wander into northern Michigan during winter.

centrations of blue jays, grosbeaks, and waterfowl. Red-throated and common loons, scoters, and whimbrels are commonly seen. After about 6 weeks of little activity, the fall migration begins in early August. For sheer numbers of birds, the fall is unrivaled as huge flights of waterfowl, shorebirds, and songbirds push southward ahead of the freezing weather. The fall migration generally brings 50,000-70,000 waterbirds past the Point. In 1991, there were 10,000 red-necked grebes alone! A few other interesting species seen here are the boreal chickadee, spruce grouse, and bald and golden eagles. If the weather holds, viewing remains good until mid-November.

Directions: From Paradise, travel north on Whitefish Road about 10 miles to Whitefish Point.

Ownership: Whitefish Point Bird Observatory (906) 492-3596

Size: 40 acres

Closest Town: Paradise

Site Description: Whitefish Point is a narrow peninsula that reaches several miles into Lake Superior toward Canada. The geography of this location makes it a natural "funnel" for migrating birds of all kinds as they pass between their northern breeding grounds and warmer wintering grounds in the South.

Wildlife Viewing: During spring and fall, Whitefish Point is one of the best birding sites in Michigan. Hawks and finches start things off in mid-March and peak in late April. During this time, up to 20,000 hawks may pass by the Point—as many as 3,000 in a single day! In spring Whitefish Point is one of the best sites in the country for owl viewing. Watch for boreal, great gray, great-horned, short-eared, and long-eared owls. The warmer days of May bring huge con-

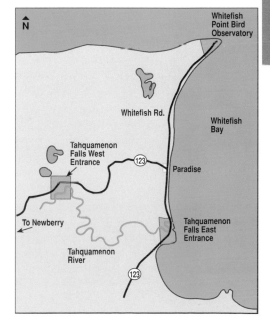

Succession: Changing Land, Changing Wildlife

To an ecologist, the term *succession* refers to the predictable changes that occur in the plants and animals that live in an area over time. See how these changes affect an abandoned Michigan farm field in the following illustrations:

1   Originally, this farm field was a deep forest filled with towering beech and maple trees. Over time the forest was cleared for farming, bringing about major changes to the kinds of plants and wildlife that could live here.

2   After several years of farming, this field was abandoned. For the next few years, annual weeds, grasses, wildflowers, and other plants invaded the bare soil, creating habitat for mice, meadowlarks, and other open field wildlife.

3   Eventually, shrubs and small trees seeded into the field. As these new plants grew, their leaves and outstretched branches shaded out the smaller plants below, creating a different kind of habitat. Chipmunks and robins were among the animals attracted to this new habitat.

4   Over time, oak and hickory trees grew tall and shaded out most of the shrubs, creating forest habitat once again. Squirrels and wild turkeys replaced chipmunks and robins in the natural chain of events. Down on the forest floor, oak and hickory seedlings struggled to grow in the shade of their forebears. Beech and maple seedlings that had seeded into the forest grew much faster in the shade, and soon stretched above the others. As the original oak and hickory trees died and fell, the spaces they left in the forest canopy were filled by beeches and maples growing up from below.

5   More than 100 years after this forest was first cleared for farming, it returned to beech-maple forest again through the process of *succession*. For this location, beech-maple forest is the *climax community*—the association of plants and animals that will remain stable until disturbed by an outside force such as fire, wind, disease, or human activity. Different regions of the world support different kinds of climax communities, including deserts, prairies, and rainforests.

Biologists use this understanding of succession to manage wildlife populations. The endangered Kirtland's warbler, for example, will only nest in stands of young jack pine trees. Periodic wildfires once maintained this habitat, but when humans suppressed fires, Kirtland's warblers had nowhere to nest and nearly became extinct. Today, in Kirtland's warbler habitat areas, managers use clearcutting and prescribed burning to prevent succession from occurring—to maintain the young jack pine habitat that the warblers and other kinds of wildlife need to survive.

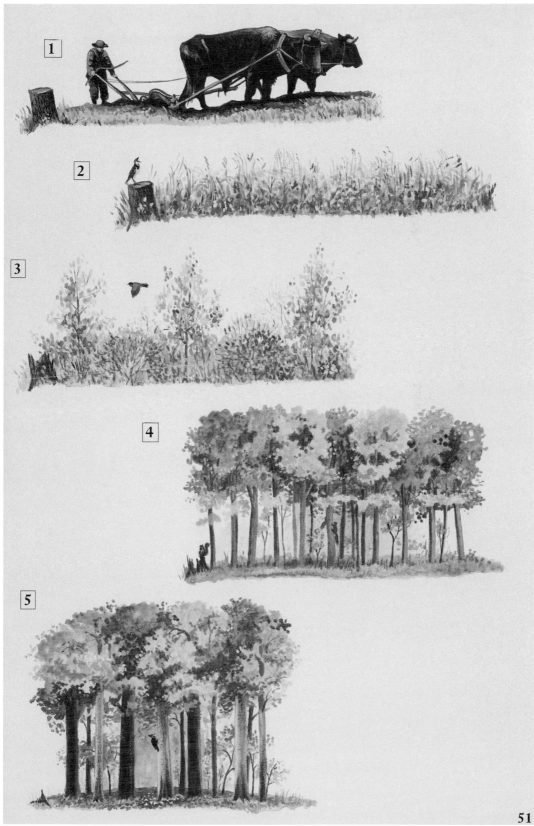

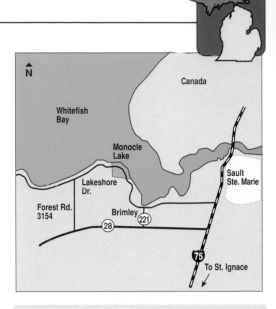

Site Description: The 2-mile hiking trail at Monocle Lake Campground passes over a nice wetland boardwalk, runs along scenic Monocle Lake, and gives access to a high bluff overlook of Lake Superior and the Canadian shoreline across the St. Marys River. The first 1,100 feet of the trail (which includes the wetland boardwalk) is fully accessible. The trail to the bluff overlook is steep and challenging.

Wildlife Viewing: The wetland boardwalk portion of the trail runs right across a beaver dam, and these industrious animals are actually using the boardwalk as part of their construction. Look for a beaver lodge in the wetland. The underwater entrances to these large stick houses allow beavers to come and go with little exposure to predators. Waterfowl also may be seen using this wetland area. There is an active osprey nest in the Monocle Lake area. Watch for ospreys (also called fish hawks) catching fish in the shallow wetland area.

PORTIONS OF THIS AREA ARE OPEN TO PUBLIC HUNTING. CONTACT THE MICHIGAN DEPARTMENT OF NATURAL RESOURCES FOR AFFECTED SEASONS AND LOCATIONS.

Directions: From Brimley, take Lakeshore Drive north about 6 miles to Monocle Lake Recreation Area on the left side of the road.

Ownership: U.S. Forest Service (906) 635-5311

Size: 2 linear miles

Closest Town: Brimley

Sporting webbed feet for power and a large, flat tail for steering, the beaver is well-suited for life in the water. With one deep breath, a beaver can remain underwater for up to 15 minutes!

Phillip Foullard

A slender, graceful duck, the pintail is a powerful flyer. Some individuals migrate from the arctic circle all the way to Central America.

Site Description: There are two primary viewing sites on this large state area. A flat, open grassland area with shallow ponds that is adjacent to the Munuscong River and a coastal marsh area on Munuscong Lake. Both of these sites are undeveloped, but some amenities are available at a nearby state forest campground.

Wildlife Viewing: A walk through the open grassland viewing site provides a good opportunity to see meadowlarks, bobolinks, and many species of waterfowl and shorebirds. Hawks also hunt for small rodents in this open area and may be seen perched in nearby trees or circling overhead. There are no designated trails through this grassland/wetland complex, but visitors are free to hike wherever they choose. This site is soggy during rainy periods, so come prepared. The coastal marsh viewing site attracts numerous waterfowl and shorebirds. Tundra swans may be seen here along with bald eagles, ospreys, muskrats, and wetland-related songbirds. The portion of coastal marsh at the primary viewing site currently is a wildlife refuge. Bring binoculars or a spotting scope to the parking area, but do not enter the marsh.

PORTIONS OF THIS AREA OUTSIDE THE REFUGE ARE OPEN TO PUBLIC HUNTING. SEE THE MICHIGAN DEPARTMENT OF NATURAL RESOURCES HUNTING GUIDE FOR SEASON DATES.

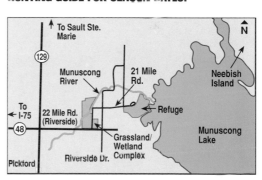

Directions: From Sault St. Marie, drive south on M-129 to 22-Mile Road (Riverside). Turn left (east) and continue 2.5 miles to the grassland viewing area on the left or continue another 1/2 mile and turn left (north) onto Riverside Drive. Proceed 1 mile and turn right (east) onto 21 Mile Road and drive 1.5 miles to the bay viewing area.

Ownership: Michigan Department of Natural Resources (906) 635-6161

Size: 15,000 acres

Closest Town: Pickford

Site Description:

Horseshoe Bay is a broad embayment of Lake Huron that lies north of St. Ignace and the Straits of Mackinac. The U.S. Forest Service administers much of the land along this bay, and the Foley Creek Forest Campground is a scenic place to sample the area's wildlife. The campground is nested among large white pine trees, providing an attractive appearance. A hiking trail on the site connects the campground with a sandy beach on Lake Huron. This campground is generally open from the end of May through the beginning of September. Call ahead for details.

Red squirrels may be found in any of Michigan's woodlands, but are perhaps most common in evergreen forests where they eat the seeds from pine cones.

Wildlife Viewing: This scenic, wooded camping area is home to white-tailed deer, raccoons, red squirrels, and many forest bird species. The one-mile linear hiking trail begins at the north end of the campground and winds through a northern white cedar swamp on its way to a sandy beach on Lake Huron. Bald eagles are sometimes seen perching in the tall white pines that face the shore. Waterfowl and great blue herons are common on Horseshoe Bay and on the small ponds that line the hiking trail. The trail provides foot access to the 3,787-acre Horseshoe Bay Wilderness.

PORTIONS OF THIS AREA ARE OPEN TO PUBLIC HUNTING. CONTACT THE MICHIGAN DEPARTMENT OF NATURAL RESOURCES FOR AFFECTED SEASONS AND LOCATIONS.

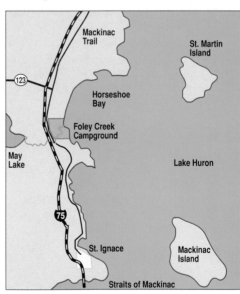

Directions: From St. Ignace, travel north on I-75 about 7 miles to the M-123 exit. Turn right (south) onto Mackinac Trail Road and continue about 1.5 miles to the entrance to Foley Creek Campground on the left side of the road.

Ownership: U.S. Forest Service (906) 643-7900

Size: 5 acre campground

Closest Town: St. Ignace

Other Wildlife Viewing Sites in the Upper Peninsula

	Site Name	County	Phone Number
1.	Laughing Whitefish Falls	Alger	906-863-9747
2.	Blind Sucker Pathway	Alger	906-293-5131
3.	Shelldrake Campground	Chippewa	906-293-5131
4.	Cartwright Farm	Chippcwa	906-478-4006
5.	Nahma Marsh	Delta	906-474-6442
6.	Lobischer Creek	Gogebic	906-358-4551
7.	Imp Lake	Gogebic	906-358-4724
8.	Lake Ottawa Campground	Iron	906-265-5139
9.	Red Pine Pit	Iron	906-265-5139
10.	US-2 Duck Ponds	Iron	906-265-5139
11.	Cooks Run Habitat Trail	Iron	906-265-5139
12.	Two Hearted River	Iron	906-265-5139
13.	Norway Lake	Iron	906-852-3500
14.	Black Creek Flooding	Mackinac	906-293-5131
15.	Hog Island Campground	Mackinac	906-293-5131
16.	Les Cheneaux Islands	Mackinac	906-484-3935
17.	Mackinac Island	Mackinac	906-847-6418
18.	McCormick Wilderness Hiking Trail	Marquettc	906-852-3500
19.	Johnson's Pond	Menominee	906-786-1660
20.	Shakey Lakes Savanna	Menominee	906-786-2354
21.	Norwich Plains	Ontonagon	906-884-2411
22.	Whitetail Deer Viewing Loop	Ontonagon	906-358-4551
23.	Courtney Lake Campground	Ontonagon	906-884-2411
24.	Mead Auto Tour	Schoolcraft	906-283-3401

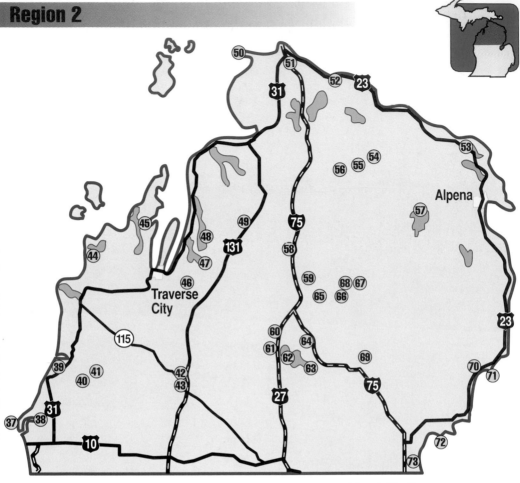

37	Ludington State Park	55	Tomahawk Creek Flooding
38	Hamlin Lake Marsh	56	Pigeon River Country Elk Range
39	Lake Bluff Audubon Center	57	Fletcher Floodwaters
40	North Country Trail	58	Deward Tract
41	Manistee River	59	Hartwick Pines State Park
42	Mitchell State Park Heritage Fisheries and Wildlife Nature Study Area	60	Fletcher Sharptail Area
		61	Dead Stream Flooding
43	Brandybrook Semiprimitive Area	62	Houghton Lake Flats—South Unit
44	Sleeping Bear Dunes National Lakeshore	63	Backus Lake
45	Suttons Bay Marsh Boardwalk	64	Marl Lake and South Higgins Lake State Park
46	Sand Lakes Quiet Area	65	Wakeley Lake
47	Skegmog Swamp Pathway	66	Luzerne Boardwalk
48	Grass River Natural Area	67	Jack Pine Wildlife Viewing Tour
49	Jordan River Valley	68	Au Sable River
50	Wilderness State Park	69	Rifle River Recreation Area
51	Mill Creek State Historic Park	70	Tuttle Marsh Wildlife Area
52	Cheboygan State Park	71	Tawas Point State Park
53	Thompson's Harbor State Park	72	Wigwam Bay Wildlife Area
54	NettieBay Lodge	73	Pinconning County Park

Site Description: Ludington State Park is practically an island, as it sits nestled between Lake Michigan and Hamlin Lake, lower Michigan's largest artificial impoundment. Here you will find lofty sand dunes, virgin stands of evergreen and hardwood trees, soft sandy beaches, and an extensive network of hiking, skiing, and canoe trails. Ludington has nearly 400 campsites that are heavily used from May through mid-October.

Wildlife Viewing: This site offers wonderful wildlife viewing opportunities from its extensive trail system. There are more than 18 miles of hiking trails, with an additional 12 miles of cross-country ski trails. Walk the Skyline Trail for some spectacular views of high dune ridges and Lake Michigan. Hike the Lighthouse Trail to Point Sable Lighthouse, administered by the Bureau of Land Mangement. Perhaps the most unique trail here is the canoe trail. Brochures at the visitor center mark a unique passage along the bayous and inlets of Hamlin Lake's shoreline. Slip silently down this trail early in the morning for a high probability of viewing herons, egrets, waterfowl, deer, and other animals along the water's edge. The

Sable River, which flows from Hamlin Lake to Lake Michigan, has some open water year round. This makes it very attractive to waterfowl from November through January.

PORTIONS OF THIS AREA ARE OPEN TO PUBLIC HUNTING. CONTACT THE MICHIGAN DEPARTMENT OF NATURAL RESOURCES FOR AFFECTED SEASONS AND LOCATIONS.

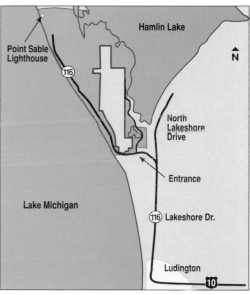

Directions: Travel west on US-10 into Ludington. Turn right (north) onto Lakeshore Drive/M-116 and proceed about 8 miles to the park entrance.

Ownership: Michigan Department of Natural Resources (616) 843-8671

Size: 5,300 acres

Closest Town: Ludington

Take a walk on Ludington State Park's Skyline Trail for spectacular views of Lake Michigan and the surrounding sand dunes.

Site Description: Located at the northern tip of Hamlin Lake, this site does not receive much use by humans, but is heavily used by wildlife. A natural, undeveloped shoreline and waves of rice grass and other wetland plants make this a quiet, peaceful place to enjoy a day of wildlife viewing.

Wildlife Viewing: A steep ridge provides a beautiful, undeveloped overlook onto the marsh. With the help of binoculars or a spotting scope there is a high probability of seeing many ducks, geese, and other wetland birds as they fly into and out of the marsh. For even better wildlife viewing, bring a canoe or boat and put in at the small gravel boat launch at the end of Forest Road 5540. Paddle silently through the tall stands of rice grass to get a close, personal look at the residents of the marsh. Muskrats, beavers, mink, great blue herons, and all manner of waterfowl make use of this area. Bald eagles are also seen occasionally. Spring and summer are the best seasons to see these majestic birds.

THIS AREA IS OPEN TO PUBLIC HUNTING. CONTACT THE MICHIGAN DEPARTMENT OF NATURAL RESOURCES FOR AFFECTED SEASONS AND LOCATIONS.

Michael M. Smith

The male wood duck is one of the most colorful of all waterfowl. Wood ducks need tree cavities for nesting. Landowners can help these beautiful birds by leaving old, dead trees standing near wetland habitats.

Directions: From Manistee, take US-31 south about 7 miles to Forest Trail (also called Michigan Road). Turn right (west) and continue 2.5 miles to Quarterline Road. Turn left (south) on Quarterline and proceed 1.5 miles to Nurnberg Road. Turn right (west) and drive 3 miles to Forest Road 5540. Turn left and drive to the parking lot at the end of the road.

Ownership: U.S. Forest Service (616) 723-2211

Size: 100 acres

Closest Town: Manistee

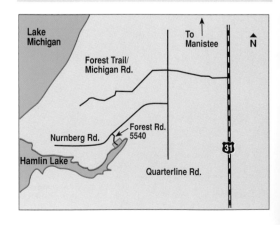

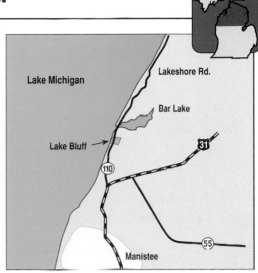

Site Description: High, rocky bluffs at this 72-acre site offer a picturesque view of the Lake Michigan shoreline and surrounding countryside. A gently rolling nature trail meanders through open field, forest, and wetland areas.

Wildlife Viewing: Lake Bluff is a good site for viewing many kinds of birds. Along the Lake Michigan shoreline during February and March, you may see concentrations of sea ducks such as oldsquaws, mergansers, and harlequin ducks. In mid-April, watch for red-tailed, broad-winged, and rough-legged hawks as they migrate north. Golden eagles and merlins are also seen occasionally. Many large, old trees reach for the skies along the nature trail, and these giants provide great feeding and nesting habitat for woodpeckers. Wild turkeys and white-tailed deer are commonly seen along the trails as well. In August, watch for large groups of monarch butterflies that stop here to rest on their long journey to Mexico. Many people are not aware that these colorful insects migrate the same as many bird species. They spend the summer months in northern latitudes and then travel south to escape the harsh winter weather.

Directions: From Manistee travel north on US-31 to M-110. Turn left onto M-110 and continue north. After about 1 mile, M-110 turns into Lakeshore Road. Lake Bluff is located on the left (east) side of the road at 2890 Lakeshore Road.

Ownership: Michigan Audubon Society (616) 889-4761

Size: 70 acres

Closest Town: Manistee

The male hooded merganser is recognized by the handsome white crest on the back of his head. Mergansers are diving ducks that have long, saw-toothed bills that help them catch and hold fish.

The yellow-rumped warbler is one of the many colorful warblers that migrate through Michigan in the spring. During fall migration, warblers wear dull, brown plumage.

Myles Willard

Directions: To Marilla Trailhead: From Brethren, drive east on Coates Highway about 7 miles. Turn left (north) on Marilla Road and continue another 7 miles. Turn right (east) onto Beers Road and proceed about 1.5 miles. Trailhead is on right side of road. To High Bridge Trailhead: From the intersection of Coates Highway and High Bridge Road in Brethren, drive south on High Bridge Road about 2.8 miles to the High Bridge Road parking lot.

Ownership: U.S. Forest Service (616) 723-2211

Size: 20 linear miles

Closest Town: Brethren

Site Description: This site is part of the North Country National Scenic Trail that when finished will extend 3,200 miles from New York to North Dakota. This 20-mile portion of the trail follows the banks of the scenic Manistee River from the Marilla trailhead to Coates Highway at High Bridge. Several trailheads along the route provide access for day trips. This trail has no facilities except for restrooms at the High Bridge trailhead.

Wildlife Viewing: Beautiful scenery and solitude await hikers who venture down this stretch of the North Country Trail. Bald eagles and osprey are often seen along the river in this area, as are deer, waterfowl, and numerous woodland songbirds. Backpack camping is permitted as long as the campsite is at least 300 feet off the trail. Listen closely in the gray light of dawn to see how many songbirds and other critters you can identify. Gray diamonds mark the trail route along with signposts at all road crossings. BRING YOUR OWN DRINKING WATER.

THIS AREA IS OPEN TO PUBLIC HUNTING. CONTACT THE MICHIGAN DEPARTMENT OF NATURAL RESOURCES FOR AFFECTED SEASONS AND LOCATIONS.

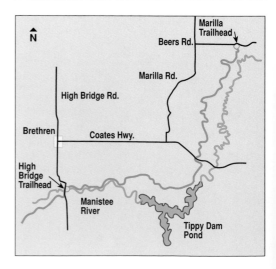

Tippy Dam and Lake Michigan the river is not as fast, but it is very scenic. The shoreline is undeveloped and the fishing and wildlife viewing are great. Deer, turkeys, eagles, raccoons, and river otters all can be seen by the careful observer. Many kinds of fish are also easily seen in the clear water.

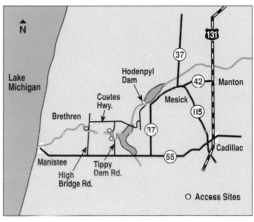

PORTIONS OF THIS AREA ARE OPEN TO PUBLIC HUNTING. CONTACT THE MICHIGAN DEPARTMENT OF NATURAL RESOURCES FOR AFFECTED SEASONS AND LOCATIONS.

A silent canoe trip down one of Michigan's scenic rivers is a great way to view wildlife. Many animals are not frightened by motorless boats, so canoes can serve as excellent viewing blinds.

Site Description: The Manistee River is one of Michigan's premier canoe floats. Clear, cool water, good fishing, and excellent wildlife watching can be found here year round. There are plenty of public access sites in the area where canoes and small boats may be launched.

Wildlife Viewing: A large concentration of ducks and geese may be seen in the waterfowl sanctuary at the head of Hodenpyl Pond just outside Mesick (drive east on M-115, then turn left onto Eugene Road and drive to the river). There is a good chance of viewing bald eagles on the 3-4 hour float between the Hodenpyl Dam and the Coates Highway bridge (Red Bridge). Osprey (also called fish hawks) can be seen snatching fish from the shallows here as well. Between

Ownership: Consumers Power Company (616) 399-3302 Extension 574

U.S. Forest Service Manistee Ranger District (616) 723-2211

Michigan Department of Natural Resources (616) 775-9727

Size: Approximately 40 river miles

Closest Towns: Manistee, Sherman, Mesick, Wellston

Hunting, Fishing, and Wildlife Conservation

Hunting and fishing have played a big role in Michigan's history. For centuries, native Americans relied on Michigan's fish and wildlife for food. With the dawn of European settlement, French voyageurs and other fur traders made their livings by hunting and trapping. The Great Lakes have supported commercial as well as sport fishing for more than a century. Today, hunters and anglers flock to Michigan to sample a wide variety of sporting opportunities.

David Kenyon

In the past, market hunting and overfishing threatened to damage Michigan fish and wildlife populations. Today, hunting and fishing are carefully regulated to protect the resource, and fish and wildlife populations are carefully monitored and managed by professional biologists.

Who pays the bills?

In Michigan and across the country, hunters and anglers pay for the majority of fish and wildlife conservation efforts, a tradition dating back to the beginning of the 20th century. They pay for it through the sale of hunting and fishing licenses and stamps, and through special excise taxes on firearms, ammunition and archery and fishing equipment. The tax programs alone have raised more than 2.2 billion dollars for wildlife conservation since their inception in 1937. This money has been used for the conservation of all wildlife—not just species that are pursued by hunters and anglers.

Phil T. Seng

When carefully regulated and scientifically managed, hunting and fishing pose no threat to fish and wildlife populations. In fact, because of license sales and tax revenues, they actually benefit these populations. For hundreds of years people have enjoyed hunting and fishing in Michigan, and there are few places that can rival Michigan in the diversity and abundance of opportunities available. With continued sound management, this proud heritage can be passed on for many more generations to come.

Site Description: Formerly used to raise northern pike for release into Lake Cadillac, this large, shallow impoundment has now reverted to marshy, wetland habitat. Dikes that encircle the impoundment create a scenic 2-mile hiking trail. Observation platforms along the trail provide nice vistas out over the marsh. This site also features a state park campground and the extensive Carl T. Johnson Hunting and Fishing Center. All buildings are barrier free.

Myles Willard

The painted turtle is the most widespread turtle in all of North America. They may be seen sunning themselves on rocks and logs throughout Michigan.

Wildlife Viewing: There is a good probability of viewing ducks, geese, herons, and other wetland-related birds—especially during spring and fall migration. Deer, beavers, muskrats, raccoons, and turtles are also very common throughout the area. Watch painted turtles sunning themselves on rocks and logs sticking up out of the water. The painted turtle is the most common turtle in Michigan and is found from the southern state line all the way to Isle Royale. The marsh trail begins behind the Carl T. Johnson Hunting and Fishing Center. Stop at this excellent facility for a fascinating and informative look at the history of hunting and fishing in Michigan.

Directions: At the junction of M-115 and M-55, travel northwest on M-115 for 0.5 miles. The state park entrance is on the right side of the road at North Boulevard. The visitor center and entrance to the nature study area are just across the canal from the park.

Ownership: Michigan Department of Natural Resources

Mitchell State Park (616) 775-7911

Carl T. Johnson Hunting and Fishing Center (616) 779-1321

Size: 235 acres

Closest Town: Cadillac

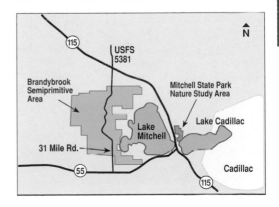

Gijsbert van Frankenhuyzen

Beavers live in lodges that they build out of sticks and pack tight with mud. These lodges have underwater entrances that allow beavers to come and go without being noticed by predators.

Site Description: Beautiful, undeveloped natural area that contains a wetland impoundment surrounded by forest. This site has no facilities or improvements, but it is adjacent to the Hemlock National Forest Campground and less than 3 miles from Mitchell State Park.

Wildlife Viewing: The waterfowl area at Brandybrook is a good place to see active beaver lodges and muskrat houses. Watch closely for the residents of these aquatic shelters at dawn and dusk. An osprey platform has been erected in the middle of the wetland. Ospreys build a nest of sticks on top of this flat, man-made platform. The same pair may use this location for many years, adding new material each year. Black bears are found at Brandybrook, and although they are rarely seen by people, their tracks, droppings, and scratch marks on trees and utility poles can be found throughout the area. It is amazing that animals this large can remain so secretive and hidden. Contrary to popular belief, bears do not hibernate during winter. They do greatly restrict their activity, spending days at a time in their dens, but they do not truly hibernate.

THIS AREA IS OPEN TO PUBLIC HUNTING. CONTACT THE MICHIGAN DEPARTMENT OF NATURAL RESOURCES FOR AFFECTED SEASONS AND LOCATIONS.

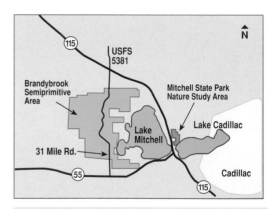

Directions: From Cadillac, drive west on M-55 about 3 miles to 31 Mile Road. Turn right (north) and continue 1.5 miles to Forest Road 5381. This road winds throughout the Brandybrook area.

Ownership: U.S. Forest Service (616) 775-8539

Size: 3,000 acres

Closest Town: Cadillac

Site Description: Large, diverse, and unique, this national park is one of the crown jewels of Michigan's natural resources. Here you will find 31 miles of Lake Michigan shoreline, including dunes, cliffs, rocky points, and protected bays. North and South Manitou Islands add another 30 miles of shoreline, and offer pristine backpacking experiences from May through October. The 7.5-mile Pierce Stocking Scenic Drive offers spectacular views of Lake Michigan, shoreline sand dunes, and the surrounding countryside. The Visitor Center in Empire provides a great introduction to the park. Don't forget to pick up maps and other materials that will make your visit more informative and enjoyable.

Wildlife Viewing: From the Pierce Stocking Scenic Drive you can see panoramic vistas as well as wildlife. White-tailed deer and wild turkeys are commonly seen along the road. Watch for groups (called kettles) of hawks soaring along the dunes in March and enjoy the colorful blooms of spring wildflowers in April and May. Float the Platte River for a good chance of seeing goldeneyes, buffleheads, and other waterfowl,

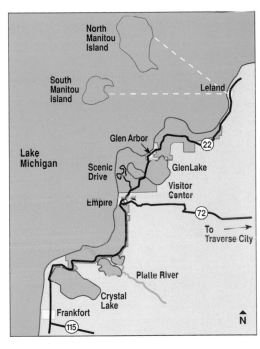

especially during spring migration. View salmon running in the clear waters of the Platte in late September and October. True to their names, Otter Creek and Otter Lake are home to river otters. Watch for these playful and energetic mammals when the ice breaks up in early April. The prairie warbler, which is a threatened species in Michigan, is commonly seen in May and June at Good Harbor Beach and Platte Bay.

Directions: From Traverse City, drive west on M-72 to the park headquarters in Empire.

Ownership: National Park Service (616) 326-5134

Size: 71,000 acres

Closest Towns: Glen Arbor, Empire

River otters are masterful swimmers that spend most of their time in or near the water. They are very sensitive to water quality and human disturbance.

45   Suttons Bay Marsh Boardwalk

Site Description: Protected from the wind and waves of Grand Traverse Bay, Suttons Bay is a haven for waterfowl and wading birds. A handicapped accessible wooden boardwalk wraps around a 7-acre, shallow-water marsh at the edge of the bay.

Wildlife Viewing: Mallards and mergansers are the most common ducks seen here, but many more use this area during spring and fall migration. Great blue herons can be seen wading in the marsh looking for the frogs and small fish that make up the bulk of their diets. Fish viewing is popular at the boardwalk bridge. Catfish, carp, and other fish are commonly seen in the clear stream water, especially in spring.

Directions: From Traverse City, drive north on M-22 about 15 miles to Suttons Bay Village. Turn right (east) onto Adams Street and follow signs to the Marina.

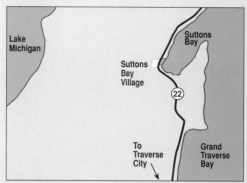

Ownership: Suttons Bay Village (616) 271-3051

Size: 7 acres

Closest Town: Suttons Bay Village

46   Sand Lakes Quiet Area

Site Description: This serene site is part of the Pere Marquette State Forest. It has five marl lakes surrounded by rolling hills of oak-pine forest. Several of the lakes are more than 40 feet deep. An extensive trail system allows visitors to explore the lakes and surrounding area on foot or skis or by bike or horse.

Wildlife Viewing: Because motorized traffic is prohibited on this site, there are ample opportunities for wildlife watchers to enjoy uncrowded trails and peaceful lakeshores. Deer, turkeys, squirrels, and other woodland wildlife are found at Sand Lakes. Several of the lakes have been stocked with test populations of hybrid fish. Call the number below for a map of the area and details on the special fishing regulations that apply to these lakes. The mud at the bottom of marl lakes contains a lot of calcium carbonate that was deposited by glaciers.

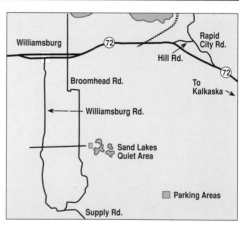

Directions: From Williamsburg, drive east on M-72 to Broomhead Road. Turn right (south) and continue about 3.5 miles to the Sand Lakes parking area on the left (east) side of the road.

Ownership: Michigan Department of Natural Resources (616) 922-5280

Size: 2,800 acres

Closest Towns: Williamsburg, Kalkaska

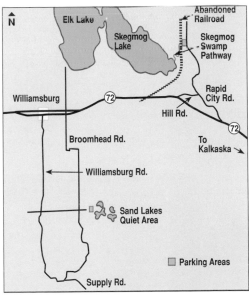

The observation platform at the end of the Skegmog Swamp Pathway offers scenic views of Skegmog Lake and the surrounding wetland area. The reclusive massasauga rattlesnake may be seen in the wetlands and moist bottomlands of this area.

Site Description: An extensive wooden boardwalk winds through a beautiful cedar swamp and crosses a small creek as it makes its way to the east end of Skegmog Lake. The boardwalk leads to an observation tower that provides a scenic view of Skegmog Lake and the surrounding wetlands.

Wildlife Viewing: The boardwalk at this site provides a unique opportunity for visitors to walk into the heart of a lush, wet cedar swamp without needing boots or waders. However, feel free to bring along wading equipment if you care to do a little exploring away from the boardwalk. The abandoned railroad grade that leads to the boardwalk is a favorite sunning location for the secretive massasauga rattlesnake—Michigan's only rattlesnake. Walk quietly and watch carefully for these small snakes basking along the grade from late spring through summer. From the boardwalk you may view herons, egrets, swamp songbirds, and other wetland wildlife. Bald eagles nest in the area and the observation tower provides a good vantage point from which they may be seen perching or fishing along Skegmog Lake.

PORTIONS OF THIS AREA ARE OPEN TO PUBLIC HUNTING. CONTACT THE MICHIGAN DEPARTMENT OF NATURAL RESOURCES FOR AFFECTED SEASONS AND LOCATIONS.

Directions: From Kalkaska, take M-72 west about 4 miles to County Road 597 (sign says "To Rapid City"). Turn right (north) and proceed about 3 miles to the parking area on the left (west) side of the road.

Ownership: Michigan Department of Natural Resources (616) 258-2711

Size: 2,700 acres

Closest Town: Williamsburg

Site Description: This site contains a well-developed network of trails, boardwalks, and observation platforms along Finch Creek and the Grass River. The trails showcase beautiful scenery and wonderful wildlife viewing opportunities starting in upland forests and leading along stream corridors then down into tamarack swamps and sedge meadows along the river. Portions of the trail are barrier free.

Wildlife Viewing: Great-horned and barred owls are common throughout this area. You can hear them hooting at night almost year round. Owls are one of the few kinds of predators that will catch and eat skunks. Like most birds, owls have a very poor sense of smell, so they are not deterred by the skunk's well-known defense. Bald eagles nest in large trees on the Grass River and they are seen frequently during the summer. Loons nest on nearby Clam Lake. Bring a canoe and float quietly along the wetlands of the Grass River down to Clam Lake. You may see a variety of aquatic wildlife on your trip including river otters, muskrats, mink, and waterfowl. A seasonal interpretive center is open from mid-June through Labor Day, and guided hikes are available. Call ahead for availability and ask for a copy of the interpretive trail brochure.

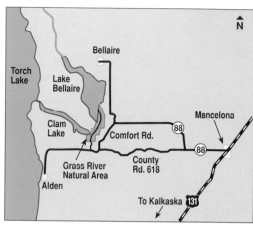

Directions: From Mancelona, drive west on M-88. After 2.5 miles, M-88 turns sharply to the right (north). Do not follow it. Instead, continue driving west on County Road 618 for about 6 miles. The site entrance is on the right side of the road, about 1/2 mile west of Comfort Road.

Ownership: Antrim County (616) 533-8314

Size: 1,100 acres

Closest Towns: Alden and Bellaire

When threatened, a great-horned owl chick spreads its wings, making itself appear as large as possible, and hisses at the intruder. By using this impressive threat display, young owls are often able to bluff their way out of danger.

The overlook at Dead Man's Hill provides spectacular views of the scenic Jordan River valley below.

Ray Rustem

the North Country Trail contact: North Country Trail Association, P.O. Box 311, White Cloud, MI 49349. Camping is only allowed at the Pinney Bridge and Graves Crossing campgrounds.

Wildlife Viewing: Good probability of seeing wetland-related wildlife throughout this area. Beavers, raccoons, frogs, turtles, herons, and waterfowl all can be seen sharing the solitude of this beautiful river corridor. Hike the trail or slowly drive the local roads for great wildlife viewing opportunities. Most of the local access is on unimproved dirt roads that are not suitable for large vehicles. The hiking trail is moderate to rugged and may be poorly marked in spots. Because of the low, wet nature of this site, spring flooding is common and black flies, deer flies, and mosquitoes can be extremely numerous in May and June. Despite these inconveniences, a trip to this beautiful area is well worth the effort.

Site Description: Good wildlife watching and beautiful scenery are common along the Jordan River—Michigan's first waterway to be classified as a Wild and Scenic River. Access to the river valley is provided by local county roads and an 18-mile hiking trail that winds through the Mackinaw State Forest. The trail contains several loops of varying lengths. One loop begins at Deadman's Hill, which also offers a spectacular vista of the river floodplain and surrounding countryside. The hiking trail is part of the North Country National Scenic Trail that when finished will extend 3,200 miles from New York to North Dakota. For more information on

PORTIONS OF THIS AREA ARE OPEN TO PUBLIC HUNTING. CONTACT THE MICHIGAN DEPARTMENT OF NATURAL RESOURCES FOR AFFECTED SEASONS AND LOCATIONS.

Directions: From Alba, drive north on US-131 about 6 miles to Deadman's Hill Road. Turn left (west) and follow the signs to Deadman's Hill Scenic Overlook (about 2 miles).

Ownership: Michigan Department of Natural Resources (517) 732-3541

Size: 16,000 acres

Closest Town: Alba

Site Description: This beautiful natural area is located on a long finger of land that protudes into Lake Michigan near the tip of the Lower Peninsula. It offers scenic views of Lake Michigan, the Straits of Mackinac, and the Mackinac Bridge. Wildlife watchers will find a campground and an extensive series of trails that provide foot travel access into the park's interior.

Wildlife Viewing: A hike in this park's interior is like a trip into the past. Stands of virgin hemlock trees and second growth Norway pines that tower nearly 100 feet into the air greet visitors to the eastern portion of the park. These large, old trees provide great nesting cavities for raccoons, owls, and woodpeckers, including the crow-sized pileated woodpeckers that are common here. Common loons and bald eagles both nest in the park. It is illegal to disturb the nest sites of either of these majestic birds. This park boasts a large population of wild orchids, including the rose pogonia, grass pink, calypso orchid, showy ram's head, and lady's slippers. Stop at the park headquarters to learn where the best blooms can be found. On winter mornings, watch for red foxes and coyotes walking on the ice of Big Stone Bay and other bays and inlets.

PORTIONS OF THIS AREA ARE OPEN TO PUBLIC HUNTING. CONTACT THE MICHIGAN DEPARTMENT OF NATURAL RESOURCES FOR AFFECTED SEASONS AND LOCATIONS.

Directions: From Mackinaw City, drive west on Central Avenue which becomes Wilderness Park Drive. A short stretch of Wilderness Park Drive is known as Trails End Road, but signs direct you toward the park. Park office is 11 miles west of Mackinaw City on the left (south) side of the road.

Ownership: Michigan Department of Natural Resources (616) 436-5381

Size: 8,000 acres

Closest Town: Carp Lake

The dwarf lake iris is a threatened species found only on or near the sand or gravel shorelines of Lake Michigan and Lake Huron. PLEASE DO NOT DISTURB.

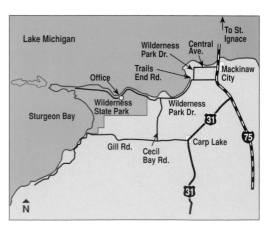

51   Mill Creek State Historic Park

Site Description: Nature trails and scenic overlooks provide a view of the wildlife and natural resources of this site, while the working sawmill and visitor center give a look at the rich history of the Straits of Mackinac and Mackinac Island. Mill Creek is open May 12 through October 17. Call ahead for a schedule of activities within the park.

Wildlife Viewing: Three miles of nature trails meander through 625 wooded acres. Hike the Beaver Pond Trail to see the dams and lodges of several groups of beavers. Watch for these shy mammals at dawn and dusk. Deer, grouse, and woodcock may be seen on the Aspen-Wildlife Forest Trail. The stubby woodcock is one of Michigan's slowest-flying birds, averaging only about 5 mph in level flight.

Directions: From Cheboygan, take US-23 north about 13 miles to the park entrance on the left (south) side of the road.

Ownership: Michigan Department of Natural Resources (616) 436-7301

Size: 625 acres

Closest Town: Mackinaw City

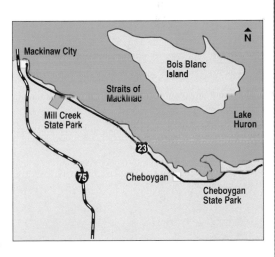

52   Cheboygan State Park

Site Description: Located along Lake Huron's Duncan Bay, this state park offers camping, hiking trails, and a diverse mixture of habitats and wildlife. There are 5-6 miles of marked hiking trails available, but some of the best wildlife viewing in the park awaits those who are willing to take a map and compass and set off on their own.

Wildlife Viewing: Located in a low, wet area along Lake Huron, this site contains a lot of swamps and wetlands. Consequently, it is a good place to see ducks, geese, egrets, and herons. Carnivorous (meat-eating) pitcher plants are common here, but you'll have to get off the trails to find them. Colorful speckled brook trout may be seen in Little Billy Elliot's Creek during late summer, and concentrations of black bass are often found in the weed beds of Duncan Bay near the campground. Bobcats are common in the park. Although these reclusive predators are rarely seen, campers sometimes hear them screaming at night. The scream is a normal call for the bobcat, but it can be unnerving if you've never heard it before.

PORTIONS OF THIS AREA ARE OPEN TO PUBLIC HUNTING. CONTACT THE MICHIGAN DEPARTMENT OF NATURAL RESOURCES FOR AFFECTED SEASONS AND LOCATIONS.

Directions: From Cheboygan drive east on US-23 four miles to the park entrance on the left (north) side of the road.

Ownership: Michigan Department of Natural Resources (616) 627-2811

Size: 1,200 acres

Closest Town: Cheboygan

What is a Food Web?

Food chains and food webs are simplified ways of looking at the way energy flows among living organisms.

It all starts with the sun, which provides the energy that sustains all life on earth.

Green plants, such as grass and duck-weed, convert the sun's energy and nutrients from the soil or water into plant material.

Herbivores (plant eaters), such as mice and minnows, eat plant materials and convert this stored energy into animal tissue.

Carnivores (meat eaters), such as hawks and bass, eat the smaller animals and transfer the energy once again.

When carnivores die, specialized organisms called decomposers con-vert this tissue back into soil nutrients that are again used by the green plants at the beginning of the chain.

In reality this diagram is oversimplified because very few animals feed at only one level of the chain. For instance, foxes eat fruits, insects, and even other small predators, which means there could be arrows connecting the carnivores with each of the other levels shown here. In addition, decomposers work at every level of the chain, adding even more arrows to this simple illustration. If all possible arrows were added, the diagram would appear more like a web than a chain, which is why these illustrations are often called food webs.

Food webs help illustrate the complex ways that energy and nutrients are transferred among living organisms and their environments. They also show how damage to any single strand can have far-reaching impacts on the health of the entire web.

Site Description:

There are no facilities or improvements at this rustic state park that includes 7 miles of Lake Huron shoreline. Primitive hiking trails wander throughout the second growth forest, sand dunes, and limestone cobble beaches of this site. Visitors are also encouraged to bring a map and compass and explore the "uncharted" portions of the park.

The fossilized remains of ancient plants and wildlife may be seen along the cobble beaches at Thompson's Harbor State Park.

Wildlife Viewing:

Much of this park's Lake Huron shoreline is covered with cobblestones that have been rounded by centuries of wind and wave action. Fossils of ancient plants and animals are common on these unique cobble beaches. Please leave the fossils behind for others to find and enjoy. There are more than 3 miles of hiking trails and old survey roads that provide access to the park's undeveloped interior. Hike these trails in late May and June to see beautiful spring wildflower blooms. The rare dwarf lake iris may be seen along the trails and on the shoreline just west of Observatory Point. Bald eagles, black bears, coyotes, and white-tailed deer all call this site home.

PORTIONS OF THIS AREA ARE OPEN TO PUBLIC HUNTING. CONTACT THE MICHIGAN DEPARTMENT OF NATURAL RESOURCES FOR AFFECTED SEASONS AND LOCATIONS.

Directions: From Rogers City, take US-23 east about 12 miles to the park entrance on the left (north) side of the road.

Ownership: Michigan Department of Natural Resources (517) 734-2543

Size: 5,300 acres

Closest Town: Rogers City

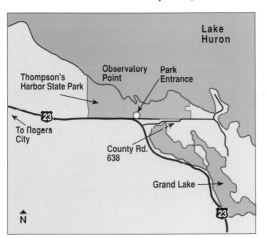

Site Description: Originally developed as a hunting and fishing lodge, this private site is now becoming well-known as a wildlife viewing destination as well. The owners can provide lodging, observation/photography blinds, and guided bird hikes on more than 2,000 acres of undeveloped wildlife habitat around Lake Nettie.

Wildlife Viewing: This site contains a diverse mixture of habitats, including upland fields and forest, wetlands, swamps, bogs, and open water lakes. Because of this habitat diversity, many different kinds of songbirds make their homes here. It is not uncommon to see more than 100 different species in a single weekend birding trip, including wood thrushes and scarlet tangers. Common loons nest on Lake Nettie and may be seen throughout the summer. Bald eagles are often seen fishing in the shallow waters of the lake. White-tailed deer, wild turkeys, coyotes, and snowshoe hares are year-round residents of this site. The snowshoe hare is named for the widely spaced toes and thick fur on its hind feet, which help support its weight on soft snow.

THIS SITE IS PRIVATE PROPERTY. YOU MUST CHECK IN AT THE LODGE BEFORE USING THE PROPERTY. CALL AHEAD FOR BEST RESULTS.

Carl R. Sams II

The brilliant red of the scarlet tanager is a color not often seen in nature. Although it gleams like a jewel in the sunlight, this secretive bird prefers to stay in the treetops and may be difficult to see.

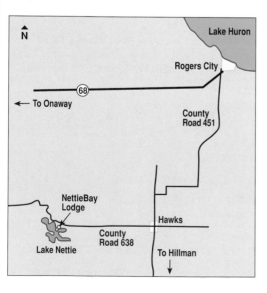

Directions: From the town of Hawks, drive west for 5 miles to the site entrance on the left (south) side of the road.

Ownership: NettieBay Lodge (517) 734-4688

Size: 2,500 acres

Closest Town: Hawks

Loons rarely venture onto land. Their legs are set at the very rear end of their bodies. This makes them excellent swimmers, but makes them very awkward on land.

Site Description: Nutrient poor, sandy soils and jack pine forest characterize this portion of the Mackinaw State Forest. Water from Tomahawk Creek has been impounded to form a broad, shallow lake that provides wonderful habitat for wetland-related wildlife. The sandy ridges and rolling hills that surround the lake are good wildlife viewing locations.

Wildlife Viewing: This peaceful setting provides the perfect backdrop for viewing nesting loons in June. Watch them from the shoreline with binoculars or a spotting scope. Do not approach or disturb nesting loons! These beautiful symbols of the North Country are very susceptible to disturbance during their nesting period. Watch for bald eagles and ospreys trying to catch fish from the shallow waters of the flooding. Ospreys, which are also called fish hawks, have long legs and talons that are specially adapted for catching fish. Eagles are not as good as ospreys at catching fish, but they are larger and often try to steal ospreys' catch.

PORTIONS OF THIS AREA ARE OPEN TO PUBLIC HUNTING. CONTACT THE MICHIGAN DEPARTMENT OF NATURAL RESOURCES FOR AFFECTED SEASONS AND LOCATIONS.

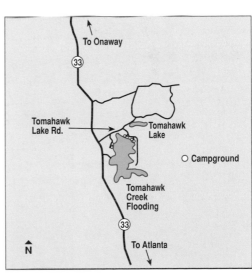

Directions: From Atlanta, drive north on M-33 about 15 miles until you see signs for the campground at Tomahawk Lake Road. Turn right (east) and follow the signs.

Ownership: Michigan Department of Natural Resources (517) 785-4251

Size: 6,000 acres

Closest Town: Atlanta

Site Description: The Pigeon River Country State Forest and surrounding land is home to the largest free-roaming elk herd east of the Mississippi River. The nearly 100,000-acre

The elk or wapiti is a large member of the deer family. Adult males may weigh up to 1/2 ton.

Mark Romesser

state forest contains native hardwoods and pines that are interspersed with fields and forest openings. The Department of Natural Resources maintains this excellent elk habitat through careful forest and wildlife management.

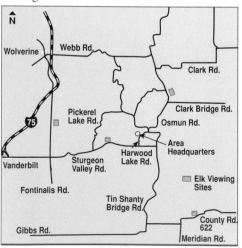

Wildlife Viewing: Elk inhabit this site year-round, but certain times are better for viewing than others. Probably the best month is September, when the males (bulls) are trying to establish dominance among themselves for mating rights with the females (cows). They are very active during this time, making loud vocalizations (bugling), and breaking brush with their antlers to impress cows and intimidate their rivals. If you plan to visit during September, try to arrive during the week. Elk viewing has become very popular and weekends are crowded. Another good time to view elk is from late April through early May. Elk are active throughout the daylight hours eating the new green growth and there are few people out to see them. Several elk viewing sites have been established on this site. These are not the only places you can see elk, but they are located in known elk gathering spots, and are good places to start. The best viewing is done from your car, since elk are accustomed to seeing cars. Use binoculars or spotting scopes for best results. Do not approach elk. Despite their large size, they are timid animals and will not tolerate much disturbance.

PORTIONS OF THIS AREA ARE OPEN TO PUBLIC HUNTING. CONTACT THE MICHIGAN DEPARTMENT OF NATURAL RESOURCES FOR AFFECTED SEASONS AND LOCATIONS.

Directions: From Vanderbilt, drive east on Sturgeon Valley Road about ten miles to one of the designated elk viewing sites. For more information, continue east about three miles to Hardwood Lake Road. Turn left (north) and continue about one mile to the Forestry Field Office. This office has maps and information about elk viewing, but hours are variable depending on the season.

Ownership: Michigan Department of Natural Resources (517) 732-3541

Size: 95,000 acres

Closest Town: Gaylord, Vanderbilt

Carl R. Sams II

With its noble, majestic appearance, the bald eagle is known throughout the world as the national symbol of the United States.

and egrets silently stalking fish and frogs in the many coves and bays along the ragged shoreline. More than 25 osprey nesting platforms have been erected in the flooding, and many of these are used each year. Do not approach nesting ospreys, but sit in your boat and watch these amazing anglers snatch fish from shallow water to feed their young. Ospreys often go into the water up to their wings, and sometimes will even plunge completely underwater to snag their next meal. On a summer evening, take a casual drive down the Farrier Road auto loop for an excellent opportunity to view large herds of deer and flocks of wild turkeys in adjacent farm fields.

Site Description: This 9,000-acre flooding along Thunder Bay River is well-known for its fishing, but it is also home to some excellent wildlife viewing opportunities. Most of the viewing here is done by boat. There is a public boat access off Jack's Landing Road if you have your own boat. Numerous private resorts along the lake provide boat rentals, camping, and other amenities. For more information contact the Elk Country Visitors Bureau at the number below.

Wildlife Viewing: This large, shallow flooding provides excellent habitat for ducks, geese, and other aquatic birds. Watch for herons

PORTIONS OF THIS AREA ARE OPEN TO PUBLIC HUNTING. CONTACT THE MICHIGAN DEPARTMENT OF NATURAL RESOURCES FOR AFFECTED SEASONS AND LOCATIONS.

Directions: For the public boat access, drive east out of Hillman on M-32 to Jack's Landing Road. Turn right (south) and continue to the Fletcher Floodwater shoreline.

Ownership: Numerous private resorts. For specific information about locations and facilities, contact the Elk Country Visitors Bureau (517) 742-4732

Size: 9,000 acre lake

Closest Town: Hillman

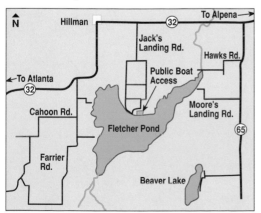

Site Description: This scenic and undeveloped tract of the Au Sable State Forest lies along the beautiful Upper Manistee River. A fishing trail in the area provides good access to the river for fishing as well as wildlife watching. A broad coalition of government agencies and private organizations has worked hard on this site to control bank erosion and maintain the river's pristine condition.

Wildlife Viewing: This stretch of the Upper Manistee River is scenic and pristine. In addition to the frogs, turtles, and trout that may be seen in the river, you also get to enjoy the great beauty of this wild, meandering river. Bring along some waders and walk gently through the riffles and eddies of this aquatic habitat. Look for deer, raccoons, and other forest wildlife crossing the river or coming to its banks for a drink. Kingfishers also may be seen here. Watch these blue-jay-size birds dive headfirst into the water to capture minnows and small fish. The surrounding forest also provides good wildlife viewing opportunities if you're willing to venture into the woods with a map and compass. Deer, wild turkeys, and woodland songbirds are common here.

PORTIONS OF THIS AREA ARE OPEN TO PUBLIC HUNTING. CONTACT THE MICHIGAN DEPARTMENT OF NATURAL RESOURCES FOR AFFECTED SEASONS AND LOCATIONS.

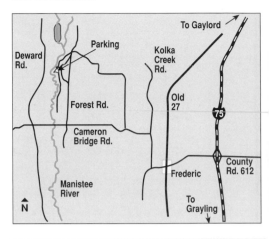

Directions: From Frederic, drive west on County Road 612 for 3/4 mile to Kolka Creek Road. Turn right (north) and proceed 1.5 miles to Cameron Bridge Road. Turn left (west) and continue 3.25 miles to a large sign at the corner of the Deward Tract. Turn right at this forest road and drive 2.6 miles to the parking area on the left.

Ownership: Michigan Department of Natural Resources (517) 348-6371

Size: 4,000 acres

Closest Town: Frederic

The green and black coloration of the leopard frog is excellent camouflage for life in the plants and mud at the water's edge.

James Harding

The visitor center at Hartwick Pines State Park surrounds visitors with the fascinating history of Michigan's lumbering era. Walk through a stand of virgin white pine trees just behind the visitor center.

Phil T. Seng

PORTIONS OF THIS AREA ARE OPEN TO PUBLIC HUNTING. CONTACT THE MICHIGAN DEPARTMENT OF NATURAL RESOURCES FOR AFFECTED SEASONS AND LOCATIONS.

Directions: From Grayling, drive north on I-75 to Exit 259. Turn north onto M-93 and proceed about 2 miles to the park entrance on the left side of the road.

Site Description: Hartwick Pines State Park is the largest state park in the Lower Peninsula. Fittingly, it also contains the largest stand of virgin white pine trees remaining in the Lower Peninsula. An extensive visitor center and logging museum help visitors explore the history of a bygone era, when most of Michigan was covered with the huge, majestic trees that still can be seen here.

Wildlife Viewing: A 50-acre stand of virgin pine trees is the premier attraction of this site. These trees were never touched by the lumberman's axe. Stroll the Virgin Pines Foot Trail and let your mind imagine how Michigan must have looked when such forest monarchs stretched from shore to shore. Because of its age, this vestige of virgin forest is gradually dying, which provides good habitat for woodpeckers. Watch for the small downy woodpecker and the crow-sized pileated woodpecker foraging for insects beneath the bark of trees along the trail. Red and black squirrels are very common in the park, and may be seen from dawn to dusk. Black squirrels are actually just a dark color phase of the gray squirrel that is common throughout the eastern United States. Stop at the visitor center for more information on the trails and other wildlife viewing opportunities available in the rest of the park.

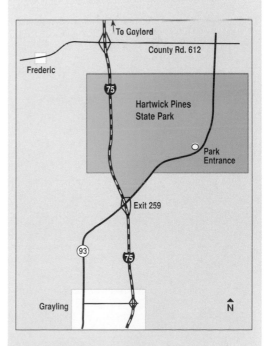

Ownership: Michigan Department of Natural Resources (517) 348-7068

Size: 9,600 acres

Closest Town: Grayling

Site Description: This open, grassy site is the last known sharptail grouse area in the Lower Peninsula. It is actively managed to maintain the open, brushy habitat required by sharptails. There are numerous unmarked trails that run throughout the area. The site has no other developments, so come prepared. Visitors are permitted to range freely throughout this unique habitat.

Wildlife Viewing: Sharptail grouse do inhabit this site, but they are rarely seen. However, other kinds of wildlife are much more cooperative. Red-tailed hawks and northern harriers (also called marsh hawks) are frequently seen hunting small rodents in the open, grassy portions of the site. Meadowlarks, horned larks, and upland sandpipers may be viewed from late spring through early fall, and vesper sparrows are extremely common.

PORTIONS OF THIS AREA ARE OPEN TO PUBLIC HUNTING. CONTACT THE MICHIGAN DEPARTMENT OF NATURAL RESOURCES FOR AFFECTED SEASONS AND LOCATIONS.

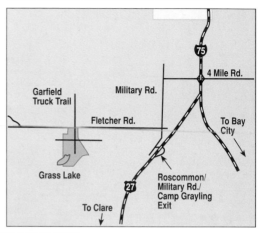

The sharptail grouse is a chicken-like bird typically found in prairie or grassland areas. Sharptails gather on breeding grounds in the spring, where males bob and strut in courtship displays.

Large numbers of deer may be seen here in the spring. Nearby Grass Lake is used by a variety of waterfowl, including a pair of nesting loons. Early summer brings an incredible grasshopper hatch. Watch songbirds and other small animals come to feed on this living carpet of insects. During the dreary days of January and February, a trip to Fletcher may be rewarded with sightings of snow buntings and snowy owls.

Directions: From Grayling, drive south on I-75 to the exit at 4 Mile Road. Turn right (west) and continue 3 miles to Military Road. Turn left (south) and proceed 4 miles to Fletcher Road. Turn right (west) and drive 7 miles to Garfield Truck Trail. Turn left (south) onto the Fletcher Sharptail Area. Driving north on US-27, take the Roscommon/Military Road/Camp Grayling Exit. Turn left (west) and proceed over the highway 1/4 mile to Military Road. Turn right (north) and proceed 1.5 miles to Fletcher Road. Turn left (west) and drive 7 miles to the Garfield Truck Trail. Turn left (south) onto the Fletcher Sharptail Area.

Ownership: Michigan Department of Natural Resources (616) 775-9727

Size: 1,200 acres

Closest Town: Grayling

Carl R Sams II

The male mallard is easily recognized by the bright green head and metallic purple wing patch (speculum). The female is mostly brown, but she too bears the purple speculum.

PLEASE DO NOT ATTEMPT TO APPROACH THE EAGLE OR OSPREY NESTS. Muskrats, mink, and river otters also make this area their home, and may be seen by the stealthy observer.

PORTIONS OF THIS AREA ARE OPEN TO PUBLIC HUNTING. CONTACT THE MICHIGAN DEPARTMENT OF NATURAL RESOURCES FOR AFFECTED SEASONS AND LOCATIONS.

Site Description: This flooding is one of the largest managed wetlands in the northern Lower Peninsula. There are no developments or improvements at this site, but the small boat ramp beckons you to a wonderful wilderness experience. The flooding is usually teeming with wildlife, and with a short trip upstream in a non-motorized boat you can explore the 30,000-acre Dead Stream Swamp—the largest semi-wilderness area in the Lower Peninsula. NO MOTORS OF ANY KIND ARE PERMITTED IN THE SWAMP.

Wildlife Viewing: The extensive beds of wild rice that grow in the flooding are very attractive to many kinds of waterfowl. Species that may be seen here include buffleheads, goldeneyes, and mallards. Scaup are also seen here in the early spring right after the ice breaks up. Spring is a great time to view waterfowl because many of them are in their bright breeding plumage. An active bald eagle nest is visible from the boat ramp and eagle viewing is very good during spring and early summer. Five osprey platforms have been placed in the flooding and most of them will be used by nesting ospreys. Ospreys are very common sightings on the flooding.

Directions: On M-55 just east of US-27 turn north on Old US-27 and drive for 2.5 miles to County Road 300. Turn left (west) and continue 1.5 miles to Michelson Road. Turn right (north) and proceed to the small parking lot at Dead Stream Flooding.

Ownership: Michigan Department of Natural Resources (517) 422-5192

Size: 2,100 acres

Closest Town: Merritt

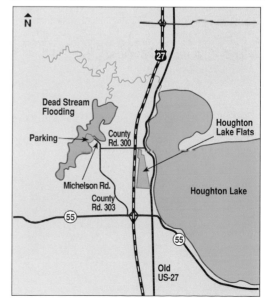

Site Description: Small, managed wetland site tucked between US-27 and Old US-27. Large birds and other wildlife in this wetland can be viewed easily from both highways, but be sure to stop at the parking area for a closer look at wildlife that don't immediately meet the eye. Houghton Lake Flats is a good place to visit when you don't have a lot of time to spend.

PORTIONS OF THIS AREA ARE OPEN TO PUBLIC HUNTING. CONTACT THE MICHIGAN DEPARTMENT OF NATURAL RESOURCES FOR AFFECTED SEASONS AND LOCATIONS.

Wildlife Viewing: These flats are lush with wetland vegetation and wildlife. A quick stop here almost anytime during the spring, summer, and fall will be rewarded with sightings of ducks, geese, great blue herons, shorebirds, and marshland songbirds. Black terns may be seen foraging in the wetland and returning to their nearby nesting colony. Two osprey nests are visible from the flats and ospreys are commonly seen fishing in the wetland. Bald eagles may also be seen flying overhead or in the vicinity. Muskrats, mink, and river otters live here year round. They are seen occasionally, usually at dawn and dusk. Use binoculars or a spotting scope from your car or take a short stroll around the wetland perimeter.

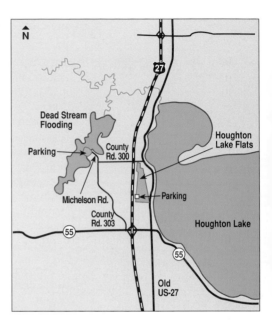

Kraig Haske

Black terns usually nest in small groups and in shallow water areas. Tern chicks leave the nest at the first sign of danger, swimming away to hide amid the surrounding wetland vegetation.

Directions: On M-55 just east of US-27 turn north on Old US-27 and drive about 1.8 miles to the small paved parking lot on the left (west) side of the road.

Ownership: Michigan Department of Natural Resources (517) 422-5192

Size: 390 acres

Closest Town: Houghton Lake Heights

Site Description: This shallow lake and the surrounding wetlands are popular with wildlife, and although the site has few amenities, it is popular with summer recreationists too. Access is limited to foot traffic only on the north side of the dam, which ensures a quiet, peaceful walk through forest, wildlife openings, and along the lake.

Wildlife Viewing: Loons nest on Backus Lake in early spring. Seeing a loon with chicks in the still morning mist is a sight not soon forgotten. Please do not approach or harass these rare and beautiful birds. The clearcuts and wildlife openings around the lake are great places to watch for wildlife. Watch and listen for male woodcocks performing their unusual courtship displays in these openings in early April. They begin on the ground, calling out a loud, nasal "peeeent" sound. Next, they launch straight up into the air and fly tight circles back to the ground, where they start over again. Coyotes are very common in this area, although they are rarely seen. An osprey nesting platform close to the road provides an excellent look at these amazing aerial anglers, and beavers have constructed a lodge of sticks in the lake near the platform.

The beautiful pileated woodpecker chisels a rectangular hole in a hollow tree to create a nesting cavity. This striking, crow-size bird is Michigan's largest woodpecker.

PORTIONS OF THIS AREA ARE OPEN TO PUBLIC HUNTING. CONTACT THE MICHIGAN DEPARTMENT OF NATURAL RESOURCES FOR AFFECTED SEASONS AND LOCATIONS.

Directions: From the intersection of M-18 and M-55 near Houghton Lake, drive north on M-18 about 1.5 miles to the junction of M-18 and M-157. Stay on M-18 but turn right (east) at the first road past this intersection. Proceed 3/4 mile to an unmarked intersection and turn left. After another 0.9 miles the road forks. Turn to the left to go to the dam or continue another 1.5 miles to the main lake area.

Ownership: Michigan Department of Natural Resources (517) 422-5192

Size: 600 acres

Closest Town: Prudenville

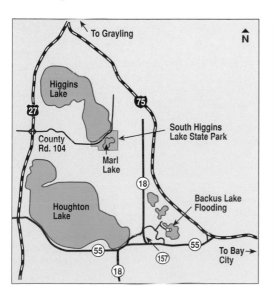

Habitat: Homes for Wildlife

David J. Case

Habitat is any place on the earth that contains everything an animal needs to survive and reproduce. This includes obvious things like food, water, air, and shelter, but it may also include many other factors such as temperature, rainfall, and soil type.

Each animal is equipped to live its life under certain conditions (the same can be said for plants). For instance, woodpeckers need dead and dying trees that provide insects to eat and soft wood for drilling nest cavities. Meadowlarks live and nest on the ground in open, grassy areas. You will not find a woodpecker perched on a fencepost in the open prairie, nor will you see a meadowlark peeking out from a nest cavity in the deep woods. The habitat just isn't right for them.

Phil T. Seng

Habitat loss is probably the greatest single problem facing wildlife today. As habitat is destroyed or altered by human activities, wildlife species are forced to find new areas of habitat, adapt to life in different types of habitat, or die. Some species are able to adapt; some become extinct.

Wildlife conservation is directly linked with habitat conservation. If habitat is available, wildlife will be there. By conserving, restoring, and creating habitat, we ensure that a variety and abundance of wildlife have places to call home.

Phil T. Seng

Site Description: South Higgins Lake State Park is nestled between Higgins Lake and Marl Lake. Here you will find trails, picnic areas, beaches, and boat ramps.

Wildlife Viewing: Marl Lake offers a good opportunity to view bald eagles. April and June are good months for this since eagles nest in the area and spend considerable time fishing here. Another bird you may see fishing in Marl Lake is the belted kingfisher. While bald eagles try to snatch fish from the water with their talons, kingfishers prefer to dive in headfirst, catching small fish in their bills. Walk the trails at the state park to view woodland songbirds.

PORTIONS OF THIS AREA ARE OPEN TO PUBLIC HUNTING. CONTACT THE MICHIGAN DEPARTMENT OF NATURAL RESOURCES FOR AFFECTED SEASONS AND LOCATIONS.

Directions: From US-27 just south of Higgins Lake, exit onto County Road 104. Turn east and proceed 6.5 miles to the entrance of Marl Lake on the right and South Higgins State Park on the left.

Ownership: Michigan Department of Natural Resources (517) 821-6374

Size: 200 acres

Closest Town: Roscommon

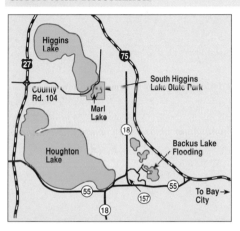

65 Wakeley Lake

Site Description: Wakeley is a shallow, marshy lake that provides good fishing and wildlife viewing opportunities. The parking lot is right off of M-72. Visitors must park and walk the 1/4-mile trail to the lake. Because motorized vehicles are not permitted, Wakeley Lake maintains a quiet, natural appearance.

Wildlife Viewing: Common loons take up residence on Wakeley Lake during spring and summer, and bald eagles come here to fish in the shallow waters. The lake has good populations of pike, bass, and sunfish that attract these birds-of-prey as well as catch-and-release anglers. Beavers and river otters make this lake their home. There are many trails and old logging roads in the forest around the lake that are open to hiking and skiing. More than 115 species of birds may be seen in this area during spring and summer.

NO BOAT MOTORS (GAS OR ELECTRIC) ARE ALLOWED ON WAKELEY LAKE. FISHING AND BOATING ARE PROHIBITED IN POSTED LOON NESTING AREAS. FISHING IS BY ARTIFICIAL LURES ONLY, AND IS ONLY OPEN FROM JUNE 15 TO AUGUST 31.

Directions: From Grayling, drive east on M-72 about 10 miles to site entrance on the left (north) side of the road.

Ownership: U.S. Forest Service (517) 826-3252

Size: 2,100

Closest Town: Grayling

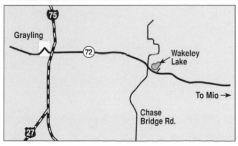

Site Description: Luzerne Boardwalk winds through an old growth cedar swamp along the east branch of Big Creek. With towering cedars overhead and water underneath, the sturdy boardwalk (constructed and used by horseback riders) offers a unique and beautiful hike. An extensive network of hiking/horse trails extends beyond the 1/2-mile boardwalk, but the boardwalk itself is not a loop trail.

Wildlife Viewing: Good birding can be found here during spring and fall migration. In the spring (April-May), American woodcocks may be heard and seen performing their mating ritual in the upland fields near the parking area. Nesting birds seen during summer include cedar waxwings, winter wrens, and black-throated green warblers. Flowers such as marsh marigold, sundew, and turtlehead can be spotted along the boardwalk. Native brook trout can be viewed on occasion from a bridge that crosses over the creek. A moss-covered opening adjacent to Big Creek 1/4 mile from the beginning of the boardwalk is a special place.

Gijsbert van Frankenhuyzen

The sundew is a highly specialized bog plant that "eats" meat. Bristly red hairs on the leaves produce droplets of sticky liquid. An insect trapped in the sticky hairs soon ends up being a meal for this unique plant.

THE TWO-TRACK ROAD AND PARKING AREA ARE ROUGH AND NARROW. CAMPERS AND RVs SHOULD AVOID THIS SITE.

Directions: From M-72 in Luzerne, drive south on Deeter Road for 1/2 mile to Palmer Road. Turn left (east) and proceed 1/4 mile to Galloway Road. Turn right (south) and drive 3/8 mile to Forest Road 3023. Turn left onto this 2-track and drive until it ends at a parking area. A horse trail on the left (north) leads from the parking area to Luzerne Boardwalk.

Ownership: U.S. Forest Service (517) 826-3252

Size: 1/2 linear mile

Closest Town: Luzerne

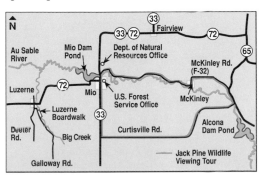

Endangered Species: Going, Going, Gone?

Piping plover

When a plant or animal species is extinct, there are no more of its kind to be found anywhere on the earth. An *endangered species* is one that is in immediate danger of becoming extinct. Extinction is not a new concept. Wildlife populations (dinosaurs, for example) were becoming extinct on the earth long before humans were around. However, humans have tremendously increased the rate at which wildlife is becoming endangered and extinct. Scientists estimate that in the eons before recorded history, one or two species became extinct about every thousand years. Today, estimates range from one species extinction per year to dozens of extinctions per day—and the rate continues to increase.

When a species is recognized as being endangered, special efforts are taken to try to save it from extinction. The trumpeter swan, piping plover, and Kirtland's warbler are good examples of Michigan wildlife that are benefitting from these special efforts. However, there are too many species on the endangered species list for all of them to get adequate attention.

Trumpeter swan

It is important to try to save endangered species from extinction. But it is even more important to prevent healthy species from ever becoming endangered. For this reason, wildlife conservation efforts are shifting away from the management of individual species toward management of ecosystems—entire communities of plants and animals that are interrelated with each other and the habitat. This is known as the conservation of biodiversity (see "Biodiversity: The Spice of Life," page 18).

Endangered species are symptoms of larger ecosytem problems. Protecting and restoring endangered species is like treating the symptoms of an illness. Conserving biodiversity is like finding the cure.

Male Kirtland's warbler

Site Description: The Jack Pine Wildlife Viewing Tour is a 48-mile auto tour loop featuring the unique jack pine ecosystem and the federally endangered Kirtland's warbler. The tour route is marked with special signs designating the route. Tour guide brochures are available at the U.S. Forest Service office, Michigan Department of Natural Resources office, and many businesses in Mio and surrounding communities. Facilities are available at various locations along the tour route.

The Kirtland's warbler is one of the most endangered birds in the country. These attractive birds require dense stands of young jack pine trees for nesting.

Wildlife Viewing: The auto tour goes through a variety of habitats and provides opportunities to see bald eagles, loons, trout, beavers, grouse, wild turkeys, and other wildlife. Specific stops along the tour offer scenic overlooks, streams and ponds, and hiking trails. The tour takes you through the nesting habitat of the federally endangered Kirtland's warbler. The entire worldwide population of Kirtland's warblers (less than 1,500 birds) nests in this part of Michigan and no where else. These small birds spend the winter in the Bahama Islands. Guided tours to see Kirtland's warblers are offered by the U.S. Fish & Wildlife Service and Department of Natural Resources in Grayling, and by the U.S. Forest Service in Mio (see phone numbers below).

KIRTLAND'S WARBLER NESTING AREAS ARE CLOSED TO PUBLIC ENTRY DURING NESTING SEASON (MAY 1 TO SEPTEMBER 10) TO PROTECT THESE BIRDS. CLOSED AREAS ARE POSTED WITH SIGNS. PLEASE DO NOT ENTER POSTED AREAS ON FOOT OR DRIVE OFF PUBLIC ROADS.

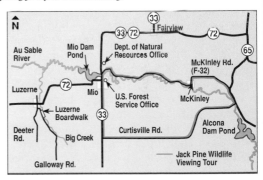

Directions: In the tour guide brochure, the tour begins by driving south out of Mio on M-33, but you can start anywhere along its route. Brochures are available at the U.S. Forest Service district office and the Michigan Department of Natural Resources office on M-33/72 north of downtown Mio.

Ownership: Michigan Department of Natural Resources (517) 826-3211
U.S. Forest Service (517) 826-3252
U.S. Fish & Wildlife Service (517) 337-6650

Size: 48 linear miles

Closest Towns: Mio, Glennie, Curtisville, McKinley, Fairview

David J. Case

A canoe float anywhere on the Au Sable River provides breathtaking scenery, excellent fishing, and plenty of wildlife viewing opportunities.

beautiful float, and there are plenty of canoe liveries available in the area if you do not have your own boat.

PORTIONS OF THIS AREA ARE OPEN TO PUBLIC HUNTING. CONTACT THE MICHIGAN DEPARTMENT OF NATURAL RESOURCES FOR AFFECTED SEASONS AND LOCATIONS.

Site Description: This stretch of the Au Sable River offers breathtaking scenery as well as excellent wildlife viewing opportunities. Panoramic vistas from cliff-top overlooks, long wooden boardwalks over spring-fed streams, and miles of quiet, undeveloped shoreline all can be found along this scenic river that flows from Grayling to Oscoda. Consumers Power Company owns and operates six hydroelectric dams along the Au Sable between Lake Huron and the city of Mio. Boat launches and canoe portages can be found at all six dams. The U.S. Forest Service and Consumers Power Company own nearly all of the river frontage in this area and they have kept the majority of this land undeveloped and open for public recreation. Contact the Forest Service for hiking, camping, skiing, and snowmobiling opportunities along the river corridor.

Wildlife Viewing: Good chance of seeing bald eagles along the river in any season. Eagles hunt for fish and waterfowl in the shallow areas of the river and in the impoundments formed by the six hydro dams. Deer and wild turkeys are plentiful along the river corridor and in the adjacent woodlands. Watch for them along roadsides at dawn and dusk. In the river, you may see trout, walleye, pike, and bass. Fishing here is excellent. The Au Sable makes an easy,

Directions: There are many access points along the Au Sable River. A good place to begin is the River Road National Scenic Byway. From Oscoda, drive west along River Road as it follows the river to M-65 and the Loud Dam Pond. Contact the U.S. Forest Service for excellent maps of the river corridor in the Huron National Forest.

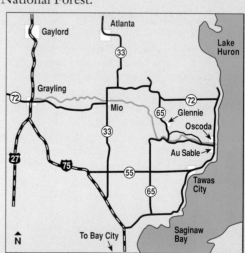

Ownership: U.S. Forest Service (517) 362-4477
Consumers Power Company

Size: Nearly 60 river miles, from Mio Pond in the west to the Foote Hydro just above Lake Huron.

Closest Towns: Mio, Glennie, Oscoda

Site Description: Water is a big attraction at Rifle River. There are more than ten miles of streams and river here, as well as 10 lakes and ponds. This site also showcases a wide variety of habitat types including upland hardwood and pine forest, open grassland, lowland forest, cedar swamp, bog, marsh, and open water. Fourteen miles of hiking/biking trails begin at the campground; many of these trails are groomed for skiers.

Wildlife Viewing: Excellent opportunity to view unique waterfowl at this site. The huge trumpeter swan, Michigan's largest bird, may be seen on any of the lakes. Trumpeters were released here by the Department of Natural Resources as part of a reintroduction program. Loons usually nest on Grebe Lake in the spring. Please view both of these rare birds from a distance and do not disturb them, especially during breeding season. A nesting colony (called a rookery) of great blue herons may be seen from the hiking trail along Skunk

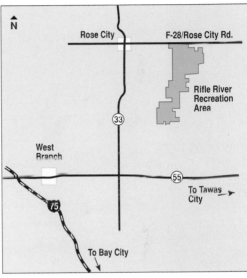

Creek. In May, the trail offers wonderful wildflower viewing. Look for Indian paintbrush, cardinal flower, several types of lady's slippers, and others. Stop at the headquarters for maps and other information.

PORTIONS OF THIS AREA ARE OPEN TO PUBLIC HUNTING. CONTACT THE MICHIGAN DEPARTMENT OF NATURAL RESOURCES FOR AFFECTED SEASONS AND LOCATIONS.

Directions: From Rose City, drive east on F-28 (Rose City Road) about 5 miles to the site entrance on the right (south) side of the road.

Ownership: Michigan Department of Natural Resources (517) 473-2258

Size: 4,500 acres

Closest Town: Rose City

Mark Picard

Great blue herons nest together in a group called a rookery. A single rookery may contain hundreds of nests.

Waterfowl

Ducks

Ducks come in many shapes and colors. Most Michigan ducks can be divided into two broad groups that are named for their eating habits.

Dabblers (also called puddle ducks) have broad, flat bills that they use to feed on plants, seeds, and insects in water less than one foot deep. They are most often seen in shallow areas of ponds, lakes, or slow-moving water. They take off from the water with a sudden, upward leap into the air.

Mallards

Divers - most diving ducks have stout bodies, short necks and tails, and large paddle feet. They dive to feed on fish, shellfish, insects, and aquatic plants. They are most often seen in open water areas of large, deep lakes and rivers. Most of them must run along the water's surface to gain enough speed to become airborne.

Bufflehead

Geese

Geese have heavier bodies and longer necks than ducks. Male and female geese look the same. Geese have strong legs that are well-suited for walking. They are grazers and spend a lot of time clipping grass and eating waste grain in farm fields far from the water.

Canada geese

Swans

Swans are the largest of all waterfowl, yet they are graceful in the air and on the water. Their bodies are all white, and males and females look alike. Their necks are longer than their bodies. Like dabbling ducks, most swans are found on ponds and lakes where they "tip up" to feed on underwater vegetation as deep as they can reach. Notice the difference between the bill of the native trumpeter swan and that of the mute swan, an ornamental swan introduced from Europe.

Trumpeter Swan

Mute swan

Site Description: A 400-acre impoundment is at the heart of this site which is surrounded by hundreds more acres of seasonally flooded wetlands. Tuttle Marsh has no facilities or developments, but visitors are encouraged to use the wetland dike as a hiking trail.

Wildlife Viewing: Thousands of waterfowl use this flooding as a feeding and resting location during their spring and fall migrations. Spring is the best time to view waterfowl here because water levels are high and ducks are in their colorful breeding plumage. Teal, goldeneyes, mallards, and Canada geese are the most commonly seen species. During summer, much of the wetland may dry up, but the impoundment still attracts herons, American bitterns, and the many shorebirds that come to feed in the exposed mud flats. During winter, large herds of deer may congregate here.

The Canada goose, with its distinctive white cheek patch, used to be a fairly rare sight in Michigan. Today, thanks to sound wildlife management techniques, Canada geese are abundant throughout the Midwest.

Vaughan Photography

PORTIONS OF THIS AREA ARE OPEN TO PUBLIC HUNTING. CONTACT THE MICHIGAN DEPARTMENT OF NATURAL RESOURCES FOR AFFECTED SEASONS AND LOCATIONS.

Directions: From Tawas City, take Monument Road north about one mile to Wilber Road. Turn right and proceed 3 miles to the stop sign at Galion Road. Turn right and drive 1/2 mile to Sherman Road. Turn left and continue 1.5 miles to May Road. Turn right and drive 1/2 mile to Brooks Road. Turn right and follow the winding gravel road for 1/5 mile to Tuttle Marsh Road on the left. Tuttle Marsh Road is about 4 miles long.

Ownership: U.S. Forest Service (517) 362-4477

Size: 4,100 acres

Closest Towns: Tawas City, East Tawas

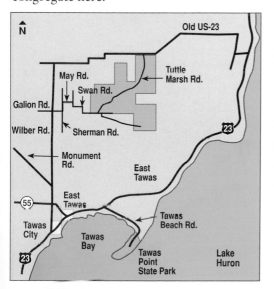

Carl Bennett

The monarch butterfly is probably recognized by more people than any other butterfly in North America. Birds and other predators quickly learn to avoid eating monarchs because their steady diet of milkweed sap makes them taste terrible.

Site Description: True to its name, this site sits on a point that sticks out into Lake Huron. Narrow, sandy beaches line both sides of the point and an interpretive trail runs from the campground to the tip of the point.

Wildlife Viewing: Because it sticks out from the surrounding shoreline, Tawas Point is attractive to waterfowl and shorebirds. See large concentrations of these birds from early March through May. Watch the Lake Huron side of the point for shorebirds and the Tawas Bay side for waterfowl. During May, you may also see other kinds of birds migrating north including broad-winged hawks, turkey vultures, warblers, and blue jays. But birds are not the only kinds of animals that migrate. In mid-August, monarch butterflies often congregate on the Point to rest as they make their annual journey south to Mexico for the winter.

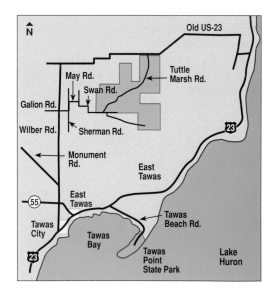

Directions: From East Tawas take US-23 north one mile to Tawas Beach Road. Turn right (east) and proceed about 2.5 miles to the park entrance on the right side of the road.

Ownership: Michigan Department of Natural Resources (517) 362-5041

Size: 200 acres

Closest Town: East Tawas

Site Description: More than 800 acres of managed wetlands occur on this relatively new state wildlife area. An extensive network of gravel-topped dikes in the wetlands is open to foot traffic all year. The remainder of the site is primarily undeveloped hardwood forest and small forest openings.

Wildlife Viewing: Wigwam Bay is an outstanding site for viewing shorebirds, waterfowl, and other wetland-related birds such as yellow-headed blackbirds, terns, and gulls. Bald eagles nest here, and are often seen soaring or sitting in perches along the dikes. Come in the spring for an excellent opportunity to see nesting snapping turtles. Although the actual nesting is usually done under cover of darkness, a walk along the dikes in early morning will often reveal the two mounds of freshly dug earth that are characteristic of snapping turtle nests. It is also common to see the remains of nests that have been pilfered by raccoons and skunks.

PORTIONS OF THIS AREA ARE OPEN TO PUBLIC HUNTING. CONTACT THE MICHIGAN DEPARTMENT OF NATURAL RESOURCES FOR AFFECTED SEASONS AND LOCATIONS.

Directions: From Standish, take Pine River Road east about 3.5 miles to Arenac State Road. Turn left (north) and drive about 1.5 miles to Stover Road (County Road 58). Continue east about 3.5 miles to the site entrance on the right.

Ownership: Michigan Department of Natural Resources (517) 426-9205

Size: 2,500 acres

Closest Towns: Standish, Au Gres

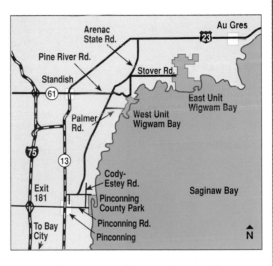

73 Pinconning County Park

Site Description: This site is a delightful yet little-known natural area that sits on the shores of Saginaw Bay. A narrow, C-shaped peninsula sticks out into the Bay creating a protected cove that is excellent for wildlife watching. Part of the site is highly developed to accommodate RV users and family camping, but there are also 4 nature trails that traverse woodlands, marshes, and the Saginaw Bay shoreline.

Wildlife Viewing: An elevated observation platform at the campground parking lot is a good place to begin your search for wildlife at Pinconning County Park. This platform provides a good view of the cattails and other shoreline vegetation that rim the small bay. Ducks, geese, and herons often congregate in this protected area. To get a closer look at them and other wetland animals, hike the Marsh Trail that runs atop the narrow peninsula. The woodland trails in the park's interior provide opportunities to see deer, squirrels, raccoons, and songbirds. The park is open April 1 - October 31. Call ahead for details.

Directions: From Bay City, take I-75 north to Exit 181. Turn right (east) onto Pinconning Road and proceed about 5 miles to the park entrance.

Ownership: Bay County Recreation Division (517) 893-5531

Size: 250 acres

Closest Town: Pinconning

Other Wildlife Viewing Sites in the Northern Lower Peninsula

	Site Name	County	Phone Number
1.	Sturgeon Point Park	Alcona	517-724-5126
2.	Negwegon State Park	Alpena/Alcona	517-724-5126
3.	Platte River Hatchery	Benzie	616-325-4611
4.	East Jordan Sportsman's Park	Charlevoix	616-536-3381
5.	Beaver Island	Charlevoix	616-547-2101
6.	Muskegon River	Muskegon	616-722-3751
7.	Camp Grayling	Crawford	517-348-3600
8.	Conners Marsh	Crawford	517-826-3211
9.	Boardman River Boardwalks	Grand Traverse	616-947-5075
10.	Rollways Campground	Iosco	517-362-4477
11.	Lumberman's Monument	Iosco	517-362-4477
12.	Olga Lake	Lake	616-775-8539
13.	Linke's Pond	Manistee	616-723-2211
14.	Tippy Dam Forest Campground	Manistee	616-723-2211
15.	Suicide Bend	Manistee	616-723-2211
16.	River Park Trail	Mason	616-757-4729
17.	Avery Lake	Montmorency	517-732-3541
18.	Ocqueoc Falls	Presque Isle	517-785-4251
19.	Presque Isle Lighthouse	Presque Isle	703-440-1668
20.	Manistee River Waterfall	Wexford	616-775-8539

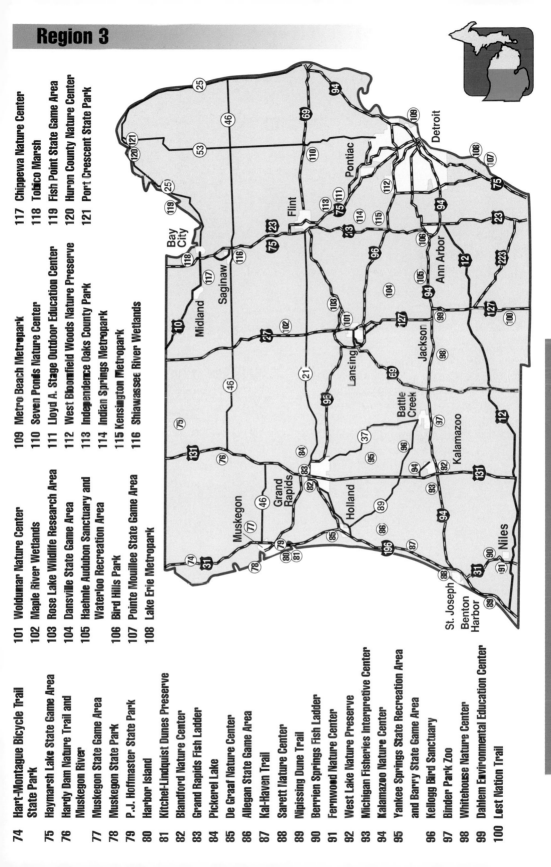

74 Hart-Montague Bicycle Trail State Park
75 Haymarsh Lake State Game Area
76 Hardy Dam Nature Trail and Muskegon River
77 Muskegon State Game Area
78 Muskegon State Park
79 P.J. Hoffmaster State Park
80 Harbor Island
81 Kitchel-Lindquist Dunes Preserve
82 Blandford Nature Center
83 Grand Rapids Fish Ladder
84 Pickerel Lake
85 De Graaf Nature Center
86 Allegan State Game Area
87 Kal-Haven Trail
88 Sarett Nature Center
89 Nipissing Dune Trail
90 Berrien Springs Fish Ladder
91 Fernwood Nature Center
92 West Lake Nature Preserve
93 Michigan Fisheries Interpretive Center
94 Kalamazoo Nature Center
95 Yankee Springs State Recreation Area and Barry State Game Area
96 Kellogg Bird Sanctuary
97 Binder Park Zoo
98 Whitehouse Nature Center
99 Dahlem Environmental Education Center
100 Lost Nation Trail

101 Woldumar Nature Center
102 Maple River Wetlands
103 Rose Lake Wildlife Research Area
104 Dansville State Game Area
105 Haehnle Audubon Sanctuary and Waterloo Recreation Area
106 Bird Hills Park
107 Pointe Mouillee State Game Area
108 Lake Erie Metropark

109 Metro Beach Metropark
110 Seven Ponds Nature Center
111 Lloyd A. Stage Outdoor Education Center
112 West Bloomfield Woods Nature Preserve
113 Independence Oaks County Park
114 Indian Springs Metropark
115 Kensington Metropark
116 Shiawassee River Wetlands

117 Chippewa Nature Center
118 Tobico Marsh
119 Fish Point State Game Area
120 Huron County Nature Center
121 Port Crescent State Park

Mark Romesser

The cardinal is a year-round resident in Michigan, and adds a splash of color and song to the sometimes dreary days of winter.

Directions: From Ludington, take US-31 south to the Hart exit. Turn left (east) onto Polk Road and proceed about one mile. The trailhead is on the left (north) side of Polk Road, near downtown Hart. From Muskegon, take US-31 north to the Whitehall exit. Travel through Whitehall and Montague to the trailhead at Stanton Street.

Site Description: This site is composed of twenty-two miles of abandoned railroad corridor that have been converted into a recreation trail. The northern portion of this paved trail is hilly and winding, while the southern segment is generally straight and flat. The trail meanders through agricultural lands, orchards, and forest, including a portion of the Manistee National Forest.

Wildlife Viewing: High probability of seeing many varieties of songbirds year-round. Moderate probability of seeing deer in fields and orchards along the trail—especially in the morning and evening. There is a great abundance of wildflowers from spring through summer. Look for remnant prairie grasses along the trail in the town of Mears. A viewing platform with picnic tables located between Mears and Shelby offers a scenic, panoramic view of East Golden Pond and the surrounding wetlands. Trail passes are required and are available from vendors in the communities along the trail.

Ownership: Michigan Department of Natural Resources (616) 873-3083

Size: 22 linear miles

Closest Towns: Major trailheads at Hart and Montague

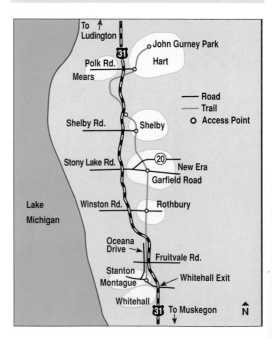

The osprey or fish hawk eats nothing but fish, which it catches by plunging feet-first into shallow water.

THIS AREA IS OPEN TO PUBLIC HUNTING. CONTACT THE MICHIGAN DEPARTMENT OF NATURAL RESOURCES FOR HUNTING SEASONS AND REGULATIONS.

Vaughan Photography

Site Description: A mixture of streams, ponds, small lakes, and wildlife floodings dot this forested area of cut-over aspen, maple, and oak. This area is primitive with few amenities. Many of the access roads are unimproved and there is only one primitive restroom. CAUTION: UNIMPROVED ROADS MAY HAVE LARGE POTHOLES OR WASHOUT AREAS. A small campground along 140th Avenue is scheduled for completion during 1994. There are numerous trails that dissect this area, but they are not marked. Feel free to hike any trails you find, but don't forget to bring a compass.

Wildlife Viewing: Excellent probability of viewing songbirds throughout the year. Haymarsh probably offers the best opportunities for viewing nesting songbirds in Mecosta County. Look for nests of golden-winged and morning warblers in May and June. Areas of overmature aspen forest provide good habitat for red-bellied woodpeckers and the large, crow-sized, pileated woodpeckers. Bald eagles and loons are seen here occasionally, and ospreys (also known as fish hawks) usually nest here in spring. September and October bring large flights of migrating Canada geese and wood ducks to the shallow water floodings of the area.

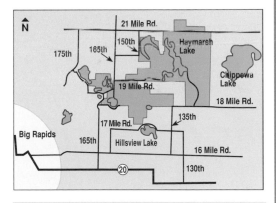

Directions: From Big Rapids, take M-20 east to 165th Avenue. Turn left (north) onto 165th. You will enter the property boundary after about 2 miles. The bulk of the area is bounded by 18 Mile Road on the south and by 21 Mile Road on the north (see map inset). Contact the Department of Natural Resources for a detailed property map.

Ownership: Michigan Department of Natural Resources (616) 832-5520

Size: 5,700 acres

Closest Town: Big Rapids

Site Description: Old-growth hardwood forest with an excellent diversity of tree species is the primary setting for this nature trail along scenic Croton Pond below the Hardy Dam. Consumers Power Company owns this land as well as a considerable amount of the Muskegon River riverfront from Big Rapids down past the Croton Dam. Most of this land is open to public use.

Wildlife Viewing: The careful observer has a good chance of seeing pileated woodpeckers along the trail. The mature forest here contains large, old trees that provide excellent

PORTIONS OF THIS AREA ARE OPEN TO PUBLIC HUNTING. CONTACT THE MICHIGAN DEPARTMENT OF NATURAL RESOURCES AND THE APPROPRIATE SITE OWNERS FOR AFFECTED AREAS, HUNTING SEASONS, AND REGULATIONS.

Directions: From White Cloud, drive south on M-37, 4.5 miles to 40th Street (USFS 5108). Turn left (east) and proceed 4.5 miles to a T. Turn left (north) and immediately turn right (east) onto 36th Street (USFS 5106). Continue about 2 miles to the parking area for the Hardy Dam Nature Trail.

Ownership: Consumers Power Company (616) 399-3302 (extension 574)

U.S. Forest Service (616) 745-4631

Michigan Department of Natural Resources (616) 856-4452.

Size: The Hardy Dam Trail area is approximately 120 acres. The Rogers, Hardy, and Croton Pond area of the Muskegon River is approximately 18 miles long.

Closest Towns: Croton, Oxbow

Tom Tietz

The porcupine is a slow and clumsy animal, but its 30,000 needle-sharp quills provide plenty of protection from most predators.

feeding and nesting areas for these showy, crow-sized woodpeckers. Deer, wild turkeys, grouse, raccoons, otters, and porcupines also are common residents of this area. Bald eagles are seen frequently along the river, and they have nested along Croton Pond. Canoes make great platforms for viewing eagles and other wildlife. The Muskegon is a scenic, enjoyable river to float, and there are portages around all three dams. To take full advantage of the lands open to the public in this area, call the site owners below for further information.

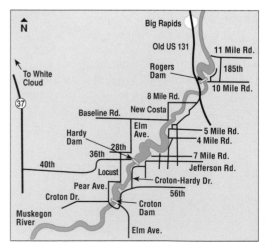

The gray tree frog is a common resident of trees and shrubs that grow in or near permanent water. Their trilling voices are often heard in spring and early summer.

Chris Doyal

river bottom flooding. Bald eagles are occasionally seen perched in dead tree snags along this trail, especially during winter. Stop at the area headquarters for a map and information on current wildlife viewing highlights.

THIS AREA IS OPEN TO PUBLIC HUNTING. CONTACT THE MICHIGAN DEPARTMENT OF NATURAL RESOURCES FOR HUNTING SEASONS AND REGULATIONS.

Directions: At the intersection of US-31 and M-46 in Muskegon, turn east on M-46 and travel 7 miles to Maple Island Road. Turn left (north) on Maple Island Road and proceed about 4 miles until you seen signs for the area headquarters. The trail access road is about one mile south of the headquarters on Maple Island Road.

Ownership: Michigan Department of Natural Resources (616) 788-5055

Size: 10,500 acres

Closest Town: Muskegon

Site Description: The scenic Muskegon River and its tributaries crisscross this 10,000-acre natural area just minutes from downtown Muskegon. The site is primarily forested, with river floodplain and wetland areas spread throughout the interior. Most of the area is not accessible by vehicles, so hikers and canoeists can enjoy an excellent wilderness experience.

Wildlife Viewing: All kinds of waterfowl are attracted to the rivers, streams, and wetlands found on this area. Mallards, blue-wing teal, and Canada geese are common. Visit during spring migration to see them in their colorful breeding plumage. There is a good dirt road off Maple Island Road south of the area headquarters that leads to a nice hiking trail. This trail follows a dike that runs through a

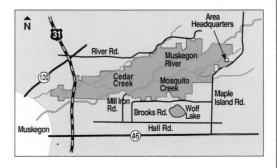

Site Description: More than 1,000 acres of scenic natural area are nestled between Muskegon Lake and Lake Michigan. This site contains dunes, interdunal ponds, forests, fields, lakefront, and a beautiful, pristine bog.

Wildlife Viewing: Because a large portion of this park is surrounded by water, it is naturally a good place to view waterfowl and shorebirds from spring through fall. Bald eagles are also seen along the lakeshores during winter. For those who enjoy unique plants, the area around Lost Lake is a gold mine. Lost Lake really is not a lake at all. It is a bog—a poorly drained and slightly acidic wetland area. Look carefully along the shores of Lost Lake and you probably will find the carnivorous (meat-eating) pitcher plant. This specialized plant is able to digest small insects to supplement the scarce nutrients available from bog soils. Please do not pick or disturb fragile bog plants.

Ring-billed gulls are common along the shorelines of the Great Lakes. These birds nest in large colonies, usually on small islands.

THE PARK IS CLOSED TO HUNTING, BUT WATER-FOWL MAY BE HUNTED ON MUSKEGON LAKE DURING THE PROPER SEASON. ALL HUNTING MUST OCCUR FROM THE WATER AND SHOOTING TOWARD THE SHORELINE IS PROHIBITED. CONTACT THE MICHIGAN DEPARTMENT OF NATURAL RESOURCES FOR HUNTING SEASONS AND REGULATIONS.

Directions: From Muskegon, go north on US-31 to M-120. Turn left (west) onto M-120, and proceed through the town of North Muskegon to the park entrance. In North Muskegon, the road name changes to Ruddiman and later to Memorial Drive.

Ownership: Michigan Department of Natural Resources (616) 744-3480

Size: 1,165 acres

Closest Town: North Muskegon

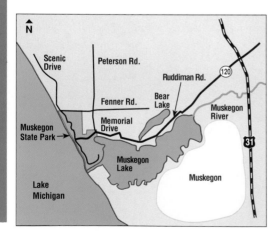

Site Description: Excellent location to see and learn about sand dune ecosystems and the wildlife that live in them. From flat beaches along Lake Michigan to a dune overlook platform perched atop a towering dune forest ridge, Hoffmaster offers a complete look at the sand dunes that stretch along Michigan's western shore. The Gillette Visitor Center is known throughout the Midwest for its outstanding programs and attractions. It was specifically designed to help visitors learn about and understand sand dune ecosystems.

Wildlife Viewing: Excellent location for viewing migrating songbirds such as wood thrushes, orioles, and tanagers. Migration occurs in both spring and fall, but viewing tends to be best during May. Songbirds that migrate from warm southern climates to northern breeding grounds try to avoid crossing Lake Michigan. Instead, they prefer to fly along the shoreline where they can stop to rest and eat in wooded areas along the way such as P.J. Hoffmaster State Park.

Directions: From Muskegon, travel south on US-31 to Pontaluna Road. Turn right (west) and follow the signs to the park entrance. If travelling north on I-96, take Exit 4 and follow signs to park entrance.

Ownership: Michigan Department of Natural Resources (616) 798-3711

Size: 1,054 acres

Closest Town: Muskegon

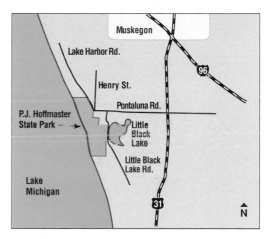

Climb the dune stairs at P.J. Hoffmaster State Park to get a bird's-eye-view of Lake Michigan and the towering sand dunes along its shores. These mountains of fine sand were created by thousands of years of wind and waves from the lake.

As its name suggests, the black-crowned night heron is active mostly at night, feeding on the fish, frogs, and other aquatic animals it finds in shallow water.

Site Description: This site is a one-hundred-forty-acre island that lies between the north and south channels of the Grand River. An operational power plant sits at one end of the island, while a marina and restaurant are located at the other end. The remainder of the island is open to wildlife viewers and other recreational users. The island contains a linear park, including a paved hiking/biking trail that offers a good view of the river channel and the undeveloped dunes on the opposite shoreline. Little-used roads on the island provide good access to viewing opportunities along the river and the associated wetlands. Parking is permitted on the shoulders of these roads except where indicated by signs.

Wildlife Viewing: Excellent opportunity to view many species of waterfowl, shorebirds, and wetland songbirds on and around the island's pond areas. Great blue herons are common

all around the island. Great egrets, terns, and a variety of gulls may be seen during spring and fall migration. European widgeons and other unique species are not uncommon, but their appearance is unpredictable. Sometimes large groups of great egrets and black-crowned night herons can be seen wading in the wetland areas adjacent to the river channels. Wildlife use of the island is determined by fluctuating water levels which are directly influenced by Lake Michigan.

THIS ISLAND IS IN THE GRAND RIVER FLOODPLAIN. OCCASIONAL FLOODING DOES OCCUR.

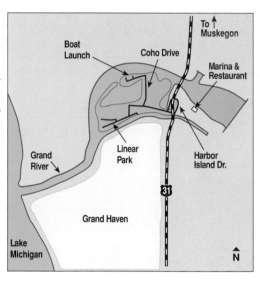

Directions: From US-31 North, turn right (east) onto Harbor Island Drive and follow the signs for Harbor Island Public Boat Launch. From US-31 South, turn right (west) onto Coho Drive and onto Harbor Island.

Ownership: City of Grand Haven (616) 842-3210

Size: 140 acres

Closest Town: Grand Haven

The Great Lakes are appropriately named, because together they form the largest body of fresh water in the world. They have a total surface area of more than 94,000 square miles—enough to completely cover Utah and still have enough left over for Connecticut, Delaware, and Rhode Island! The two peninsulas which form the state of Michigan are nearly surrounded by these "sweet water seas." The lakes have tremendous impact on the state's climate and the wildlife species found here.

During winter, these huge lakes become very cold. Air moving cross the lakes in April and May is cooled by the chilly water before it reaches land, delaying the onset of spring in the land near shore. By the end of summer the opposite is true— the warm lakes slow the progress of autumn in lakeshore areas. These lake effects give Michigan a slightly different climate than neighboring states.

Centuries of constant wave action on the shores have formed spectacular sand dunes on the western side of the Lower Peninsula and along the windward shores of the Upper Peninsula. These dunes support several plant and wildlife species found only in the Great Lakes area.

European explorers used the lakes' easy access to the interior of North America. Exploration of the lakes and connecting rivers began in the mid-1600s as a potential route to the Pacific Ocean. Over the years, ease of commercial transportation transformed the Great Lakes region into a major industrial area. Many shipping ports here were among the busiest in the world.

Michigan's geology provides numerous recreational opportunities. The variety of ecosystems and abundance of water has made this state a destination spot for campers, hikers, anglers, hunters, wildlife watchers, and photographers throughout the world. Michigan truly is, as the motto proclaims, the Great Lakes State.

The blue racer is an extremely fast and agile snake that may grow to be more than 6 feet in length. Racers eat mice, frogs, small birds, and even other snakes.

large numbers of hawks during their fall migration in September and October. Watch for hawks on days when there is an east wind blowing. Excellent chance of seeing ring-billed gulls, herring gulls, great blue herons, and other water birds. Warblers, woodpeckers, sparrows, swallows, and many other songbirds can be seen at various times from spring through fall. Dawn and dusk provide the best viewing opportunities. Several kinds of reptiles including hognose and blue racer snakes may be seen during summer.

Site Description: Excellent example of a sand dune ecosystem. This site contains all stages of dune development, from bare beach areas along the Grand River to climax dune forest. Two trails wind through the interdunal area and along the Grand River shoreline. This site is undeveloped and has few amenities, so come prepared.

Wildlife Viewing: Many different kinds of birds use this area. Excellent probability of viewing

Directions: From Muskegon, drive north on US-31 to the Ferrysburg exit. Turn right (west) on Third Street. Third Street bears to the right, becoming 174th Avenue. Turn left from 174th onto North Shore Road. Follow North Shore about 2 miles to Lake Michigan, where it bears south and becomes North Shore Drive. Continue 1 mile and turn left (east) onto Berwyck. The entrance to the preserve is immediately on the left. Park along the shoulder of Berwyck.

Ownership: City of Ferrysburg (616) 842-5950

Size: 112 acres

Closest Town: Grand Haven

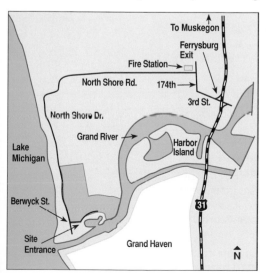

The screech owl is a small owl of the open, hardwood forest. It is dependent on hollow trees or bird boxes for nesting.

Site Description: This site contains a diverse mixture of rolling hardwood forest, streams, ponds, wetlands, and old farm fields just minutes from downtown Grand Rapids. Hiking trails wind throughout all of the habitats found on this 143-acre preserve. Portions of the trail are barrier free.

Wildlife Viewing: Excellent chance of seeing nesting great-horned owls from an observation deck just behind the Visitor Center. The best time for viewing them is in April and May. These owls may also be seen hunting fox squirrels near their nest at dawn and dusk. Screech owls are common here too and, although they are rarely seen, they often can be heard "screeching" on summer nights. Forested portions of the preserve offer magnificent wildflower viewing in the spring, and chorus frogs and spring peepers add music to spring evenings. Blandford houses an active wildlife rehabilitation unit, and animals that cannot be returned to the wild may be viewed in enclosures near the Visitor Center. The Visitor Center is open Monday through Friday from 9 a.m. to 5 p.m. and on weekends from 1 to 5 p.m. Hiking trails are open every day from dawn to dusk.

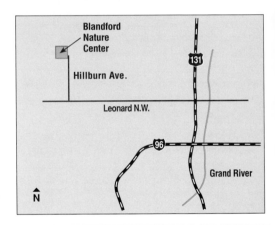

Directions: From US-131 in Grand Rapids, take the Leonard Street exit and travel west for about 3 1/2 miles to Hillburn. Turn right (north) on Hillburn to reach the nature center at the end of the street.

Ownership: Administered by the Public Museum of Grand Rapids (616) 453-6192

Size: 143 acres

Closest Town: Grand Rapids

83   Grand Rapids Fish Ladder

Site Description: The Sixth Street dam near downtown Grand Rapids prevents migratory fish such as salmon and steelhead from moving up and down the Grand River. However, on the west side of the river, a series of stair-step concrete pools called a fish ladder has been constructed to allow these fish to bypass the dam on their journey upstream toward Lansing. A specially designed viewing structure allows visitors to see fish as they pass by. Parking is available adjacent to the fish ladder and also nearby on the street.

Wildlife Viewing: The fish ladder at this site was designed and built with fish viewing in mind. Visitors can view several fish species put on quite a show as they "climb" the ladder by jumping from pool to pool. Large steelhead may be seen at this site in the spring, while coho and chinook salmon are best viewed in early fall. Other species such as carp might be viewed here any time of year. Carp are very vigorous jumpers that provide spectacular entertainment.

Directions: From US-131 in Grand Rapids, take the Leonard Street Exit. Drive east on Leonard to Front Street. Turn right (south) and continue to the end of the street. Turn left (east) into the parking lot next to the fish ladder.

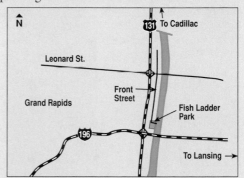

Ownership: City of Grand Rapids (616) 456-3216

Size: 1 acre

Closest Town: Grand Rapids

84   Pickerel Lake

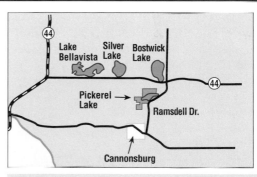

Site Description: Seventy-two acre lake with undeveloped shoreline and 163 acres of surrounding land. Site includes wetland areas, shrubby uplands, several small ponds, oak-hickory woodlots, and a unique larch swamp that is the only one of its size remaining in Kent County.

Wildlife Viewing: Songbird viewing is very good throughout the shrubby areas of this site, and small mammals such as squirrels, rabbits, and chipmunks are also common. A large population of white-tailed deer live around the lake and are often seen, especially in winter. In the lake and wetland areas, look for raccoons, herons, and waterfowl. From the wetland boardwalk you can view an active beaver lodge. Beavers and muskrats are often seen swimming in the lake. Dawn and dusk are the best times to watch for them.

Directions: From Village of Cannonsburg just northeast of Grand Rapids, travel east 1/4 mile on Cannonsburg Road to Ramsdell Drive. Turn north (left) and drive about one mile to Pickerel Lake.

Ownership: Kent County Parks (616) 336-3697

Size: 235 acres

Closest Town: Cannonsburg

Site Description: This small but unique nature center in the city of Holland provides a close look at several of Michigan's natural communities, including forest, wetland, pond, creek, and meadow. The Helen O. Brower Interpretive Center describes and interprets these communities and the animals that live here.

Wildlife Viewing: A barrier-free trail winds throughout the nature center grounds. Walk the trail early in the morning for a fair-to-good chance of viewing white-tailed deer, cottontail rabbits, and raccoons. In early May, 25-30 kinds of warblers can be seen here during their migration to northern breeding grounds. The banks of the permanent creek that runs through the property are often covered with animal tracks. See if you can match the tracks to the animals that made them. Stop by the interpretive center if you need help with the tracks and to learn more about the animals that made them.

Mark Romesser

The eastern box turtle is the only Michigan turtle that spends its entire life on land. Box turtles may live to be 100 years old, and the female may lay fertile eggs for up to 4 years after a single successful mating.

Directions: From I-196 or US-31 in Holland, take the 16th Street Exit. Turn west onto 16th and travel through town. Sixteenth eventually joins 17th and the name changes to Southshore Drive. Continue one block to Graafschap Road. Turn left (south) onto Graafschap and proceed 5 blocks to the nature center on the right (west) side of the road.

Ownership: City of Holland (616) 396-2739

Size: 15.5 acres

Closest Town: Holland

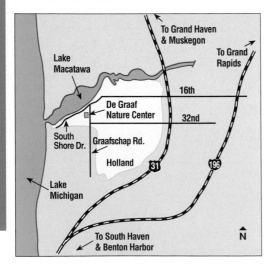

Site Description: Wonderful wildlife viewing opportunities abound in this 50,000-acre state game area. Allegan is a showcase for oak-pine barrens (also called oak-pine savanna)—a unique community of plants and animals adapted to life on the dry, sandy soils of this area. Allegan also features lowland hardwood and oak-pine forests, wetlands, ponds, and open fields.

Wildlife Viewing: Perhaps the most dramatic wildlife viewing opportunity at Allegan is the mass concentration of Canada geese that assembles here in the fall. More than 100,000 geese will pass through the area and as many as 40,000 may be seen at one time. Best viewing is in the Fennville Farm Unit on the southwestern boundary of the property. Fennville includes a refuge unit where no human access is allowed, but viewing from the road is excellent. Fennville is also a good place to see deer at dawn and dusk. The unique oak-pine barren/savanna communities and some restored prairie fields may be viewed from

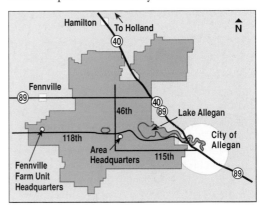

along M-89 or from any of the county roads that crisscross Allegan. Some of these openings are commonly used as hunting areas by raptors (birds-of-prey). Bald eagles and golden eagles may be seen on the area during migration. Look for the dark phase of the rough-legged hawk from December through February. Go to the area headquarters for maps and for more information on the current wildlife viewing hotspots.

THIS AREA IS OPEN TO PUBLIC HUNTING. CHECK WITH THE MICHIGAN DEPARTMENT OF NATURAL RESOURCES FOR HUNTING SEASONS AND REGULATIONS.

Directions: Travelling north on M-89 in the city of Allegan, turn left (west) onto Monroe Road (118th Avenue) and proceed 7 miles to the area headquarters.

Ownership: Michigan Department of Natural Resources (616) 673-2430.

Size: 50,000 acres

Closest Towns: Allegan, Fennville, Hamilton

The American kestrel is Michigan's smallest falcon. These jay-sized birds are commonly seen perched on telephone lines along highways, where they scout for insects and small rodents in the median.

Site Description: This site contains thirty-eight miles of abandoned railroad corridor that have been converted to a hiking/biking trail between Kalamazoo and South Haven. The trail traverses forests, agricultural lands, open fields, streams, and 11 towns and cities. It crosses 7 bridges that provide scenic views of rivers, streams, and the surrounding countryside.

Wildlife Viewing: Portions of the trail offer a good chance of seeing squirrels, chipmunks, woodchucks, and rabbits from spring through fall. Raccoons, opossums, and red foxes are seen occasionally, especially at dawn and dusk. Look for their tracks in the snow during winter. Songbirds such as cardinals and chickadees can be seen year-round, while bluebirds are common in spring and summer. Nearly 80 bluebird nesting boxes have been erected along the trail in the open field habitat that bluebirds require.

Directions to Kalamazoo terminus: From Kalamazoo, take M-43 West to 10th Street. Turn right onto 10th Street and travel about one mile to the parking area on the left side of the street.

Directions to South Haven terminus: From Van Buren State Park, take the Blue Star Memorial Highway north about 6 miles until you see signs for the trail. Turn right into the parking lot.

Ownership: Michigan Department of Natural Resources. Administered by Van Buren State Park (616) 637-4984. Funding, operation, and maintenance provided by Friends of the Kal-Haven Trail.

Size: 38 linear miles

Closest Towns: Kalamazoo and South Haven (trail endpoints)

Carl R. Sams II

Although it spends most of its time on the ground, the eastern chipmunk may be seen scurrying to the top of tall oak trees to gather ripe acorns.

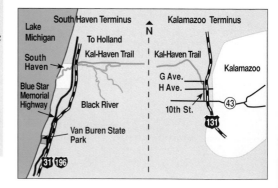

Michael M. Smith

The bright red cardinal flower is usually found along streams and other wet areas. These vivid tubular flowers are pollinated mostly by hummingbirds.

Site Description: Nearly five miles of trails, including boardwalks and observation platforms, meander through this unique, 500-acre nature center. One of the trails is barrier free. Trails that run atop the Paw Paw River bluffs provide great views of the river valley below, and boardwalks down in the floodplain give an up-close look at wetland habitats and wildlife—all without getting your feet wet. This site also contains a unique alkaline wetland called a fen.

Wildlife Viewing: Bird viewing is excellent along all of the trails. The trail system begins at the visitor center. Be sure to stop at the visitor center to pick up a trail map and look out the viewing windows. These windows offer a panoramic view of wetlands and forest in the river bottom below. A complex of feeders at the windows attracts numerous songbirds and small mammals year-round. As many as 20 male cardinals have been seen here at one time! Wildflower viewing at Sarett is spectacular. Walk the Gentian Loop Trail in August and September to see fringed gentians, turtle heads, pitcher plants, and cardinal flowers. Try the Waxwing Loop Trail in May for spring wildflower viewing. During fall migration, sit in the West Marsh Tower at dusk to view large concentrations of wood ducks and other waterfowl.

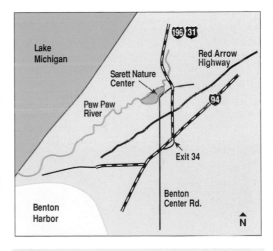

Directions: From Benton Harbor, take I-94 east to Exit 34. Follow I-196/US-31 North to Red Arrow Highway. Turn left (west) and continue 1/8 mile to Benton Center Road. Turn right (north) and proceed 3/4 mile. Nature center entrance is on the left (west) side of the road.

Ownership: Sarett Nature Center
(616) 927-4832
Michigan Audubon Society

Size: 500 acres

Closest Town: Benton Harbor

Site Description: Three hiking trails begin at the Cook Energy Information Center and amble through coastal, lowland, and dune forests; across dune meadow and blowout areas; and down into an interdunal wetland area. PORTIONS OF THE WETLAND TRAIL MAY BE CLOSED FOR CONSTRUCTION. CALL AHEAD FOR INFORMATION. An overlook platform built high on a dune ridge provides a scenic view of Lake Michigan and the beach below. Trails are open Tuesday-Sunday, 10 a.m. to 5 p.m. Closed holidays.

Viewing Information: These dune trails are perfect for a quick, peaceful get-away. Chipmunks, red and gray squirrels, and forest songbirds are often active around the visitor center and along the trails. Red foxes and woodchucks live here, but these secretive animals are rarely seen. Look for woodchuck dens along the trails. White-tailed deer are common at this site. When snow is on the ground, you will see their many trails crisscrossing the dunes. From the lake overlook platform, watch gulls and waterfowl on Lake Michigan. The warm water plume from the Cook Nuclear Power Plant keeps a portion of the lake open all winter, attracting waterfowl to bathe and feed.

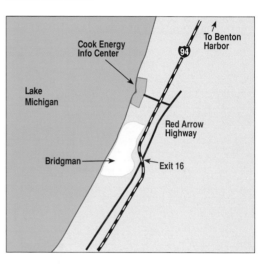

Directions: From Benton Harbor, drive south on I-94 to Exit 16 at Bridgman. Turn left (north) onto Red Arrow Highway and drive 3.5 miles to the Cook Energy Information Center entrance on the left (west) side of the road. Drive to the Cook Center and follow the signs to the nature trails.

Ownership: Indiana Michigan Power Company (800) 548-2555

Size: 10 acres

Closest Town: Bridgman

Gray squirrels are very common in hardwood or mixed forests throughout the eastern United States. These small mammals do not hibernate, instead they depend on buried nuts to see them through the winter.

John Trout Jr.

Site Description: This series of stair-step pools allows trout, salmon, and other fish to swim around the hydroelectric power dam that spans the St. Joseph River as they migrate upstream. This site is undeveloped and there are no facilities, although it is located near downtown Berrien Springs.

Wildlife Viewing: This site is an excellent place to view fish, big fish. Amazingly, there are fish moving through this ladder almost every month of the year. Steelhead are the most common, and may be viewed from June through April. To see the greatest variety and numbers of fish, come to the ladder in September and October. The fall run brings chinook and coho salmon, brown trout, steelhead, and even walleye, smallmouth, and carp through the ladder. In the spring, you may see loons in the pool above the dam. Bald eagles and osprey may be seen fishing in the waters below the dam.

Directions: From Benton Harbor, take US-31 south into Berrien Springs. Drive downtown to the stoplight at West Ferry Street and turn left. Proceed one block and turn right onto South Main Street. Continue 5 blocks to Oak Street and turn left. Drive to a 'T' intersection and turn right onto a dirt road. A small parking area for the ladder will be immediately on your left.

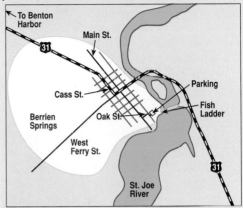

Ownership: Michigan Dept. of Natural Resources (616) 685-6851 Indiana Michigan Power Company

Size: 1 acre

Closest Town: Berrien Springs

91   Fernwood Nature Center

Site Description: Fernwood is dominated by moist soil hardwood forest leading down to the banks of the St. Joseph River. Three to five miles of hiking trails pass by numerous springs and seeps. This site also features botanical gardens and a restored prairie.

Wildlife Viewing: High probability of viewing songbirds and small mammals at the nature center feeding station year-round. Bluebirds are plentiful in open areas during summer. The harmless and beneficial black rat snake (threatened in Michigan) is commonly seen throughout the property. Spring wildflower viewing is excellent, and prairie flowers are outstanding from July through the first frost. Visit the nature center to see the displays on local wildlife and to pick up brochures for the self-guided nature trails. Educational programs are offered year-round, but the nature center hours are seasonal. Call ahead for details.

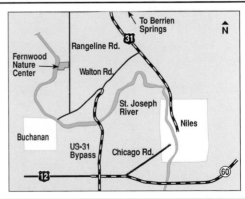

Directions: From US-31 Bypass, take Walton Road Exit west to Rangeline Road. Turn right (north) and travel 2 miles to Fernwood entrance on the left side of the road.

Ownership: Fernwood Botanic Garden (616) 695-6491

Size: 105 acres

Closest Town: Buchanan

Site Description: A large and unique sphagnum bog is the highlight of this site. Trails and boardwalks carry visitors from dry upland forest areas through lowland forest, swamp, and finally onto the floating mat of sphagnum moss that grows in the bog. A special boardwalk network actually "floats" right on top of this dense mat of moss. DURING TIMES OF HIGH WATER, YOUR FEET MAY GET SLIGHTLY WET ON THIS BOARDWALK.

Wildlife Viewing: Bogs are home to some strange plants and animals that are highly specialized for life in a wet, acidic environment. One of these is the carnivorous (meat-eating) pitcher plant, which is fairly common here. The pitcher plant has specialized leaves which look like small pitchers or vases. These leaves collect and hold rainwater. When the plant's fragrant nectar attracts insects, they become trapped in tiny hairs and drown in the pitchers, where they are digested with special enzymes. Other unique plants found here include bladderwort, pink lady's slipper, leatherleaf, and bog cranberry. Contact the Portage Department of Parks and Recreation for their Wander the Wetlands brochure that explains more about this rare and unusual bog community.

David J. Case

Insects captured by the meat-eating pitcher plant provide nitrogen and other nutrients that allow these unique plants to grow in the harsh bog environment.

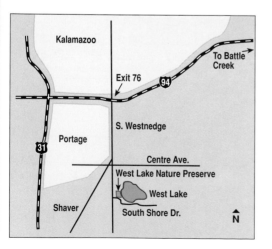

Directions: From I-94 in Kalamazoo, take Exit 76. Travel south on South Westnedge for 3 miles to South Shore Drive. Turn left (east) onto South Shore and look for site entrance on the left side of the road.

Ownership: City of Portage
(616) 329-4522

Size: 130 acres

Closest Town: Portage

Coho salmon work their way up one of Michigan's cool, clear streams. The Wolf Lake State Fish Hatchery supplies trout and salmon fingerlings to rivers and streams throughout the state.

Directions: From the junction of M-43 and US-131 in Kalamazoo, take M-43 west about 6 miles to the large hatchery road signs. Turn left (south) on Hatchery Road and proceed to the second drive on the right which leads to the interpretive center.

Site Description: This 7,000 square foot interpretive center offers visitors a fascinating look at Michigan's fish and fisheries management efforts. The Center is located on the grounds of the Wolf Lake State Fish Hatchery, just eight miles west of Kalamazoo. Completed in 1983, this modern facility and the adjacent show pond provide great adventure for anyone interested in the diverse assortment of fish that call the Great Lakes State home. No entry fee required.

Wildlife Viewing: Visitors can view an assortment of the fish found in Michigan from the show pond. A long observation platform provides close viewing opportunities into the clear water of the pond. Inside the modern interpretive center, you can learn about all aspects of fisheries science through displays, multi-media programs, and interpretive materials. Learn about the habits and biology of fish, as well as the history of fishing in Michigan—from native Americans to the present.

NOTICE: GENERALLY OPEN WEDNESDAY-SATURDAY FROM 10-5, FROM JUNE THROUGH OCTOBER, ALSO OPEN SUNDAYS 12-5. CALL AHEAD FOR SEASONAL CHANGES.

Ownership: Michigan Department of Natural Resources (616) 668-2876

Size: 7,000 square feet

Closest Town: Kalamazoo

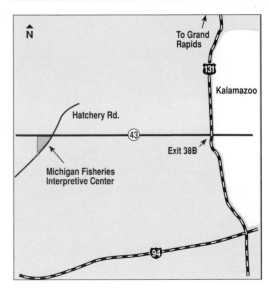

Birds-of-Prey (Raptors)

Eagles

Bald eagle

Eagles are large-bodied birds with large, broad wings, short tails, and heavy, curved bills. The white head and tail of the adult bald eagle is unmistakable, but juveniles are mottled brown and white.

Red-tailed hawk

Hawks

Hawks come in many shapes and sizes. The commonly-seen red-tailed hawk is recognized in flight by its large body, rounded wings, and fanned red tail. Watch for them perching on trees and fenceposts along Michigan's highways.

Falcons

Falcons are streamlined birds that have long, pointed wings and fairly long tails. The blue jay-size American kestrel (also called sparrow hawk) is the smallest American falcon. These handsome birds are commonly seen on telephone lines along roadways.

American kestrel

Vultures

Vultures (also called buzzards) are large birds with extremely long, broad wings and no feathers on their heads or necks. The turkey vulture is easily recognized in flight by the way it holds its wings in a V-shape and glides in wide, lazy circles.

Turkey vulture

118

Site Description: Mature beech-maple forest, wetlands, ponds, streams, open fields, and reconstructed prairie all can be found in this educational nature center just north of downtown Kalamazoo. Originally preserved to prevent gravel mining in the beech-maple forest, this site now boasts an extensive interpretive center, human environments (historical) area, arboretum, trail network, and a butterfly/hummingbird garden.

also has a fair-to-good chance of seeing muskrats and snakes. The Beechwood Trail winds among massive beech and maple trees that stand as monuments to a bygone era. The Bluebird Trail offers excellent opportunities to view bluebirds, and ends at a beautiful overlook of the Kalamazoo River Valley. During fall migration, you may see large kettles (groups or "flocks") of hawks soaring above the valley. Many colorful critters are attracted to the butterfly/hummingbird garden and arboretum in the center of the grounds.

Directions: From Kalamazoo, travel north on US-131 to Exit 44 for D Avenue. Turn right (east) and continue three miles to Westnedge Avenue. Turn right (south) onto Westnedge. The site entrance is about one mile south of D Avenue on the left (east) side of Westnedge.

Ownership: Kalamazoo Nature Center (616) 381-1574

Size: 1,016 acres

Closest Town: Kalamazoo

Wildlife Viewing: A nice variety of songbirds and small mammals can be seen at the interpretive center viewing window year-round. While you're there, ask for trail maps and some of the other excellent educational materials available. Walk the Marsh Trail to the pond and along the Trout Run stream for excellent probability of viewing frogs, turtles, and aquatic insects. The quiet, stealthy hiker

Phil T. Seng

Car Bennett

The Kalamazoo Nature Center's Bluebird Trail ends at this scenic overlook of the Kalamazoo River valley. The tiger swallowtail and other butterflies are common throughout the Nature Center during summer.

119

Scotty Lovett

Male wild turkeys fan their tails and strut during the spring mating season. Their booming gobbles are a welcome sound in the spring woods.

wildlife openings and food plots. An entry fee is required to use Yankee Springs State Recreation Area.

Wildlife Viewing: White-tailed deer and wild turkeys are common on both areas and the winter months offer excellent viewing opportunities. On Yankee Springs, take the Long Lake Trail to view waterfowl and wading birds such as great blue herons. This trail also contains a scenic wetland boardwalk. On Barry, watch for sandhill cranes in and around the northern section of the property. Warbler viewing on Barry during spring migration is also very good. Visitors may travel and park along any roads on both properties unless otherwise marked. Stop at either property headquarters for maps of the areas.

BARRY AND PORTIONS OF YANKEE SPRINGS ARE OPEN TO PUBLIC HUNTING. CONTACT EITHER PROPERTY HEADQUARTERS FOR HUNTING SEASONS AND REGULATIONS.

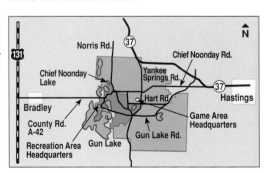

Site Description: When combined, these two adjoining Michigan Department of Natural Resources properties total more than 22,000 acres of rolling, forested hills, pine plantations, shrubby old fields, wildlife openings, wetlands, and small lakes and ponds. Yankee Springs has campgrounds, beach areas, and five hiking trails that wind throughout the park and along scenic Gun Lake. Barry is less developed and is actively managed for upland wildlife such as ruffed grouse, wild turkey, cottontail rabbits, and a multitude of songbirds and other wildlife. These species require a mixture of woodlands, grasslands, and agricultural fields to survive. Management practices on Barry include periodic timber harvesting to maintain openings throughout the area and the maintenance of

Directions: From US-131 South, turn east at the Bradley exit and proceed along County Road A-42 to Gun Lake Road. Follow the signs to the Yankee Springs Headquarters.

Ownership: Michigan Department of Natural Resources (616) 795-9081 (Yankee Springs Headquarters)

Size: Yankee Springs State Recreation Area: 5,000 acres

Barry State Game Area: 17,000 acres

Closest Town: Hastings

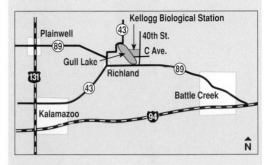

Site Description: In the 1920s this area consisted of highly eroded cropland, but it has since been restored to include woodlands, brushy areas, prairie, wetlands, and a lake. The visitor center, most of the trails, and the lakefront are barrier free. This sanctuary, which is a unit of Kellogg Biological Station of Michigan State University, is open seven days a week.

Wildlife Viewing: The outstanding feature of this site is the number and variety of waterfowl that can be seen. Hundreds of ducks, geese, and swans make this site their year-round home, with thousands more spending part of their year here. During October and November, you may see more than 20 different kinds of waterfowl on Wintergreen Lake as they stop to feed and rest on their long journey south. Fair-to-good chance of seeing the threatened trumpeter swan here from November through February. The trumpeter is Michigan's largest native waterfowl species. Males may weigh as much as 38 pounds and have wingspans of nearly 8 feet! Kellogg also is a good area to see songbirds during the spring migration. A flock of more than 100 black ducks spends the winter here, taking advantage of the open water on Evergreen Lake.

Directions: From Battle Creek, take M-89 west to 40th Street. Turn right (north) and travel 1.5 miles to C Avenue. Turn left (west) onto C Avenue. Entrance is first driveway on the right (north) side of the road.

Ownership: Michigan State University (616) 671-2510

Size: 3,600 acres

Closest Town: Hickory Corners

The largest species of waterfowl in Michigan is the trumpeter swan. Although it had vanished from the state, citizen contributions to the nongame income tax check-off have been used to reintroduce this graceful, elegant bird to our skies and waters.

Like many birds that forage for insects, the white-breasted nuthatch is often seen creeping about on the bark of trees. However, few other birds can move down the trunk of a tree headfirst.

Site Description: Zoos generally are not included in the *Michigan Wildlife Viewing Guide* because the focus of this book is on native, free-roaming wildlife. However, Binder Park offers more than animal exhibits. Fewer than 100 of the park's 405 acres have been developed as a traditional zoo. The remainder consists of forests, fields, and an extensive wetland area. Trails that traverse these areas allow visitors to experience the native wildlife in natural habitats. Some of the 8-mile trail system—including a wetlands encounter trail—is still under construction and should be completed by 1996. Hiking trails are free, while there is an admittance charge for the zoo and the wetlands encounter trail.

Wildlife Viewing: In the forested areas, look for white-tailed deer, squirrels, chipmunks, and songbirds. Fowler's toads are very common from spring through fall. In the wetland, there is a high probability of viewing muskrats, Canada geese, mallards, great blue herons, northern water snakes, and painted turtles. The painted turtle is Michigan's most common turtle, and may be seen basking on rocks and floating logs throughout the state.

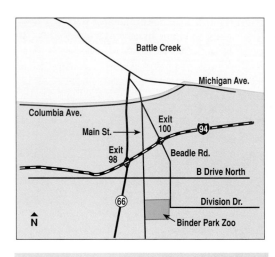

Directions: From I-94 in Battle Creek, take Exit 100 (Beadle Lake Road.) Travel south on Beadle Lake Road about 3 miles to the zoo entrance on the right.

Ownership: Binder Park Zoological Society, Inc. (616) 979-1351

Size: 405 acres

Closest Town: Battle Creek

Site Description: Four self-guided nature trails provide good wildlife viewing opportunities in woodland, wetland, old field, and prairie habitats in this 135-acre nature center. This site offers scenic vistas along the East Branch of the Kalamazoo River, a summer butterfly garden, and an arboretum that showcases Michigan trees and shrubs.

Phil T. Seng

The trails at Whitehouse Nature Center provide good opportunities to view wildlife and scenic habitat along the East Branch of the Kalamazoo River.

Wildlife Viewing: Whitehouse provides many excellent birding opportunities. More than 175 species of birds have been seen here. Look for great blue herons, green herons, and kingfishers in the wetlands. Waterfowl viewing is also good here, especially in spring and fall. The interpretive center has a feeding window that attracts numerous birds and small mammals. It also attracts Cooper's and sharp-shinned hawks that may be seen trying to make a meal of the other feeder patrons. A bridge over the river gives an excellent vantage point for fish viewing in the clear water. Look for spawning beds on the gravel bottom during early summer. Be sure to see the viewing window and pick up the trail brochures available in the interpretive center.

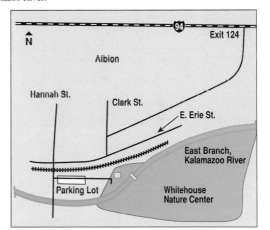

Directions: From I-94, take Exit 124 to Albion. Travel to the traffic light at Clark Street and turn left. Follow Clark to a T intersection at East Erie Street. Turn right and continue to Hannah Street. Turn left onto Hannah, cross the RR tracks, and immediately turn left again into the parking lot. Follow signs through the parking lot to the nature center.

Ownership: Albion College (517) 629-2030

Size: 135 acres

Closest Town: Albion

The bluebird may be the best-loved Michigan songbird. Bluebirds require tree cavities for nesting and raising their young, but they will readily use nest boxes if natural cavities are not available.

year! The best time for bluebird viewing is between April 15 and July 31, when adults are busy feeding the young. Bluebirds require cavities for nesting, and they readily use the nest boxes that have been erected throughout this site. A good variety of tree species along the trails makes for excellent fall color hikes. Feeders at the visitor center attract many songbirds and small mammals during winter.

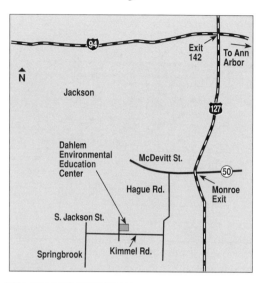

Site Description: Five miles of hiking trails wind through mature forest, brushy old field, prairie, and wetland on this gently rolling site. A wooden boardwalk allows hikers to get out into the middle of the wetland. A portion of the trail system is barrier free.

Wildlife Viewing: In the spring, the trails are great for viewing trilliums and other wildflowers. Nearby Jackson Community College is home of the annual Bluebird Festival held the first weekend in March. This area boasts one of the most successful bluebird management programs in the country—more than 500 young birds are fledged each

Directions: From I-94 in Jackson, take Exit 142 onto US-127 south and drive to the Monroe exit. Turn left (west) onto McDevitt Street and proceed to the first stoplight. Turn left (south) onto Hague Road and continue to Kimmel Road. Turn right (west) onto Kimmel and right again onto South Jackson Road and follow the signs to the site entrance.

Ownership: Jackson Community College (517) 782-3453

Size: 333 acres (250 acres accessible)

Closest Town: Jackson

Site Description: Located on the 2,500-acre Lost Nation State Game Area, the Lost Nation Trail is an old county road that has been closed to vehicles. It winds through hardwood forest, brushy areas, and wetlands along the St. Joseph River bottomlands. The trail is 1.5 miles in length and is barrier free throughout. TRAIL MAY BE FLOODED IN SOME AREAS DURING PERIODS OF HEAVY RAIN. This site is undeveloped and has no facilities, so come prepared.

Wildlife Viewing: Wild turkeys are common throughout this area. Look for them in fields along the roads. In the spring, listen for the loud, excited gobbles of male turkeys at dawn and dusk. This site is probably the only place in southcentral Michigan that offers a fair chance of seeing or hearing ruffed grouse. Listen for their characteristic "drumming" sound in the spring. The males make this sound with their wings to establish a breeding territory and to attract females. The endangered Kirtland's watersnake is also found here, although this timid reptile is rarely seen.

Kraig Haske

The ruffed grouse is named for the black "ruffs" on the sides of its neck. In spring the male sits on a log, puffs up his chest, and beats the air with its wings. This creates a drumming sound that can be heard over long distances.

PORTIONS OF THIS AREA ARE OPEN TO PUBLIC HUNTING. CONTACT THE MICHIGAN DEPARTMENT OF NATURAL RESOURCES FOR HUNTING SEASONS AND REGULATIONS.

Directions: From M-34 in Pittsford, travel west for 2 miles to Tripp Road. Turn left (south) and drive 0.3 mile to the parking area on the left (east) side of Tripp Road.

Ownership: Michigan Department of Natural Resources (517) 522-4097

Size: 1.5 linear miles

Closest Town: Pittsford

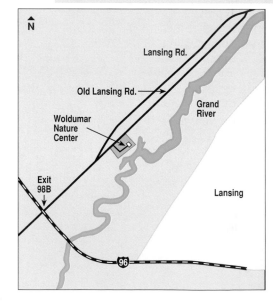

Tom J. Ulrich

At fewer than 4 inches long, the ruby-throated hummingbird is the smallest bird in Michigan. These tiny birds can flap their wings at an incredible 6,000 times per minute!

Carl R. Sams II

The bright yellow American goldfinch has also been called the wild canary. These attractive birds eat mostly seeds, so they do not nest until late summer when weed seeds are readily available.

Directions: From I-96 in Lansing, take Exit 98B and turn north onto Lansing Road. Proceed about 3 miles and bear right onto Old Lansing Road. Look for signs at the site entrance.

Ownership: Nature Way Association (517) 322-0030

Size: 188 acres

Closest Town: Lansing

Site Description: Woldumar contains nearly 200 acres of natural beauty just minutes from the bustle of downtown Lansing. More than three miles of trails lead visitors through hardwood forest, pine and spruce plantations, old apple orchards, ponds, fields, wetland, and along the banks of the Grand River.

Wildlife Viewing: White-tailed deer are common at Woldumar—in the fall they are attracted to the apples still produced at the old farm orchard. Deer can run 35 miles per hour over short distances, and are able to leap up to 8 feet off the ground! Songbird viewing is excellent year-round. Nearly 150 different kinds of birds can be found here at some time during the year. Ducks and geese are commonly seen in the pond, the marsh, and along the Grand River. Stop at the interpretive center to pick up a trail map and other materials.

Site Description: The Maple River State Game Area contains the largest contiguous wetland complex in mid-Michigan. It primarily consists of floodplain, lowlands, and marshes associated with the Maple River corridor. The eastern end of the area has been divided into 4 wildlife management units (A-D). These units are easily accessed by US-27 and offer prime wildlife viewing.

Wildlife Viewing: Wetland-related wildlife may be viewed here year-round. Spring waterfowl viewing is excellent, as thousands of ducks, geese, and swans stop over in these wetlands on their annual migration to northern breeding grounds. Viewing is best from March through May. A large rookery or nesting colony of great blue herons can be easily seen in the tops of flooded trees in Unit A just west of US-27. Hike along the dikes in this unit for a good look at these beautiful wading birds and their young. Bring binoculars for best viewing. Herons are extremely plentiful throughout the area. Fair probability of seeing bald eagles and osprey perched on dead snags in area wetlands. A wildlife observation tower and barrier-free viewing blind located in Unit B provide wonderful views of the floodplain/wetland complex. See the area map at the parking lot on US-27 for more detail.

Directions: From Lansing, take US-27 north past St. Johns to the Maple River crossing. Just past the river is the sign for the parking lot on the right (east) side of the road.

Ownership: Michigan Department of Natural Resources (517) 373-9358

Size: 9,000 acres

Closest Town: St. Johns, Ithaca

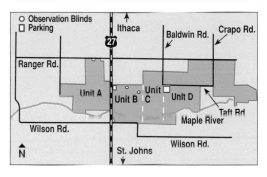

THIS AREA IS OPEN TO PUBLIC HUNTING. CHECK WITH THE MICHIGAN DEPARTMENT OF NATURAL RESOURCES FOR HUNTING SEASONS AND REGULATIONS.

Wetlands and floodplains along the Maple River are home to waterfowl and many other kinds of wetland wildlife. Except for tropical rainforests, wetlands are the most productive habitats in the world.

What is a Wetland?

True to its name, a wetland contains land that is wet, although it may not be wet year round. Most wetlands are associated with shallow water and aquatic plants. Michigan has four basic types of wetlands:

David J. Case

Marsh - contains fresh water and small aquatic plants such as cattails, water lilies, and lotus.

Swamp - contains fresh water and a few small plants, but is dominated by shrubs and trees.

Bog - contains acidic water created by decaying plants and an absence of fresh water in-flow. Bogs may have floating mats of dense sphagnum moss and other specialized plants.

Fen - the rarest of Michigan's wetlands, fens contain alkaline water that flows from caves and other underground water supplies. Fens are very fragile and are easily disturbed.

Nationwide, wetlands are home to more different kinds of wildlife than any other type of habitat, and nearly half of all U.S. endangered species depend on wetlands for survival.

In addition to being tremendous wildlife habitat, wetlands also provide many other services that are directly beneficial to people including:

Water quality - wetlands dramatically increase water quality by trapping soil that erodes from the land and by removing organic wastes and many disease agents from the water.

Flood control - wetlands serve as giant sponges, storing rainwater and releasing it gradually to storm-swollen streams and rivers.

Groundwater recharge - wetlands purify and replenish the wells that provide many people with drinking water.

Recreation - a healthy wetland can provide tremendous recreational opportunities for hunters, birders, and other outdoor enthusiasts.

In days gone by, people believed that wetlands were unproductive "wastelands," and nearly 75% of Michigan's original wetlands have been drained for agriculture or development. Today we understand that wetlands are brimming with life and are extremely beneficial to society. Protecting and restoring wetlands has become a conservation priority—in Michigan and throughout the world.

Site Description: Once a working farm, this site now contains a diverse mixture of habitats including lakes, wetlands, old fields, and forest. Work roads that double as hiking/biking trails traverse the area. The topography is flat to gently rolling.

Wildlife Viewing: Because of the diversity of habitats found here, many different kinds of wildlife may be viewed at Rose Lake. A great variety and abundance of songbirds are seen here. Sandhill cranes are known to nest here and may be seen flying to and from nesting marshes from May through August. Great blue herons are seen commonly in the lakes and wetland areas, and American bitterns also may be seen by the careful observer. Bitterns are small, elusive wading birds with brown striped necks. When approached, they will stand erect, aim their pointed bills straight upward, and blend right in with the sedges, cattails, and other aquatic plants that give them refuge.

THIS AREA IS OPEN TO PUBLIC HUNTING. PLEASE CHECK AT THE AREA HEADQUARTERS FOR HUNTING SEASONS AND REGULATIONS.

Directions: From Lansing, travel east on I-69 North to the East Lansing exit and turn left (west) onto Old M-78. Continue about 1/2 mile to Upton Road. Turn left onto Upton and proceed to Stoll Road. Turn right onto Stoll and drive about 1/4 mile to the area headquarters.

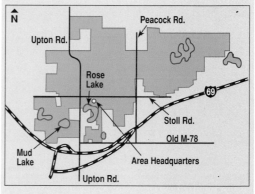

Ownership: Michigan Department of Natural Resources (517) 373-9358

Size: 3,646 acres

Closest Town: Bath

The American bittern is a small, brown heron that leads a secretive life in dense marsh vegetation. Although it is rarely seen, its loud, pumping call may be heard from a half mile away.

The male ring-necked pheasant is an extremely handsome bird. Pheasants have adapted well to agricultural areas in Michigan and throughout the American Great Plains.

Site Description: Dansville is a gently rolling area that contains forest, brushy old fields, and several small lakes. Foot paths and 2-track roads crisscross the site and provide good hiking access to the interior portion of the property. This site is undeveloped and has no facilities, so come prepared.

Wildlife Viewing: Ring-necked pheasants, bobolinks, and meadowlarks are common in the grassy upland areas of this site. All of these birds build their nests right on the ground. Wild turkeys and white-tailed deer are also plentiful. Wading birds such as herons and egrets may be viewed on the lakes and wetland, and waterfowl viewing is especially good in the spring when ducks are in their breeding plumage. Call the number below for a map of the area, or stop by the pheasant hatchery on Hawley Road.

THIS AREA IS OPEN TO PUBLIC HUNTING. CHECK WITH THE MICHIGAN DEPARTMENT OF NATURAL RESOURCES FOR HUNTING SEASONS AND REGULATIONS.

Directions: From Lansing, take US-127 south to Kipp Road Exit. Turn left (east) onto Kipp Road and travel to a T intersection at Dexter Trail Road. Turn right and proceed to Hawley Road. turn right (south) onto Hawley and drive 1/2 mile to the Property Headquarters on the left.

Ownership: Michigan Department of Natural Resources (517) 625-4600

Size: 5,000 acres

Closest Town: Dansville

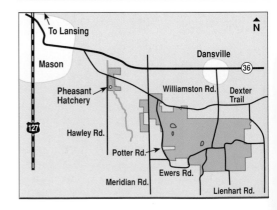

Like formations of large aircraft, sandhill cranes set their wings and glide in for a landing against the autumn sunset. Cranes rely on waste grain in harvested farm fields for the energy they need to migrate to Georgia and Florida for the winter.

Mark Romesser

A large concentration of cranes seen on a frosty October morning will be a memory not soon forgotten!

PORTIONS OF WATERLOO ARE OPEN TO PUBLIC HUNTING. CHECK WITH THE MICHIGAN DEPARTMENT OF NATURAL RESOURCES FOR HUNTING SEASONS AND REGULATIONS. HUNTING ON THE HAEHNLE SANCTUARY IS PROHIBITED.

Directions: From Ann Arbor, take I-94 west. Take Exit 156 and follow the highway signs to Waterloo State Recreation Area headquarters. For the Haehnle Sanctuary, follow I-94 to Exit 147. Turn right (north) on Race Road and proceed about 2 miles to Seymour Road. Turn left (west) and continue about 1 mile to the entrance of the Sanctuary which is on the right. CAUTION: SITE ENTRANCE IS A PARTIALLY HIDDEN DRIVE. USE CAUTION WHEN ENTERING AND EXITING FROM SEYMOUR ROAD.

Site Description: The majority of the Haehnle Sanctuary was once farmland that has now been restored to wildlife habitat. Young forest, shrubby fields, wet meadows, and open wetlands dominate the area. This site has few facilities and is intended for low impact recreational use at no cost to visitors. The Waterloo Recreation Area comprises more than 20,000 acres of rolling woodlands, old pastures, wetlands, and lakes. Portions of this area are highly developed and used, but much of the area receives little attention. Waterloo offers camping, skiing, horse trails, bike trails, and more than 30 miles of hiking trails.

Wildlife Viewing: The primary attraction of this area is the fall migration of sandhill cranes. As many as 2,000 of these large wading birds can be seen in the wetland areas of Haehnle Sanctuary in the mornings and evenings from late September through early November. This is the largest concentration of cranes in Michigan. By driving the county roads through Waterloo and within 5 miles of Haehnle, you may discover large flocks of cranes feasting on waste grain in local farm fields. Michigan's tallest bird, the sandhill crane stands about 4 feet tall, with a wingspan of 6 feet. More than 200 other kinds of birds have also been sighted in this area, including the rare black tern that nests at the sanctuary.

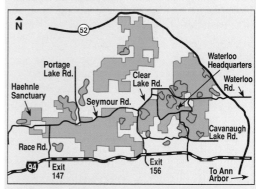

Ownership: Haehnle Sanctuary: Michigan Audubon Society (517) 769-6891

Waterloo Recreation Area: Michigan Department of Natural Resources (313) 475-8307

Size: Haehnle Sanctuary: nearly 1,000 acres Waterloo Recreation Area: 22,000 acres

Closest Town: Grass Lake

Site Description: Large, old trees cover rolling hills and steep ravines that lead down to the banks of the Huron River near downtown Ann Arbor. This 150-acre haven is criss-crossed with numerous hiking trails that can easily make you think you're a long way from the confines of the bustling city. This site is undeveloped, but water and facilities are just moments away in Ann Arbor.

Directions: From M-14 in Ann Arbor, exit onto Miller Road and travel east (toward the downtown area) to Newport Road. Turn left (north) onto Newport and proceed 3/4 of a mile to the site entrance on the right.

Ownership: Ann Arbor Department of Parks and Recreation (313) 994-2780

Size: 151 acres

Closest Town: Ann Arbor

Kraig Haske

The black squirrel is actually just a dark color phase of the eastern gray squirrel and is fairly common throughout Michigan.

Wildlife Viewing: Good probability of viewing white-tailed deer along the trails at dawn and dusk. Black squirrels are also common. The black squirrel is actually an alternate color phase of the gray squirrel that is found throughout Michigan. The state record sugar maple tree can be found in Bird Hills Park, along with numerous other very large, old, hardwood trees. Old trees are very attractive to woodpeckers and other birds that feast on the insects that live under the bark and in dead, decaying limbs. Barton Park, which is slightly northeast of Bird Hills Park, offers a hiking trail that crosses the Huron River and follows a railroad corridor.

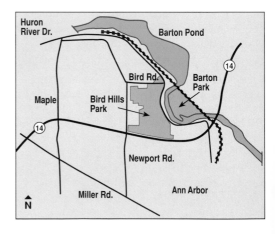

Site Description: Pointe Mouillee (pronounced "Point Moo-yay") is a spit of land that juts into Lake Erie near the mouth of the Huron River. It consists of wetlands, diked marshes, and river bayous. The wetland dikes make excellent hiking/biking trails, although visitors should be aware that construction and maintenance traffic occurs throughout the year. Site maps are available at the area headquarters.

Wildlife Viewing: Waterbirds and other wetland wildlife are the primary attraction at this site. Walk or ride a bike along the water control dikes for a good look at muskrats, waterfowl, shorebirds, wading birds, and birds-of-prey. This area provides some of the best shorebird viewing in the state, especially in late summer and early fall. There are many different kinds of shorebirds, and many of them look alike. Bring along a good field manual to help you get the most out of your trip. Call the Audubon Rare Bird Alert (810) 477-1360 for updates on unusual sightings in this area.

MOST OF THIS AREA IS OPEN TO PUBLIC HUNTING. CHECK WITH THE MICHIGAN DEPARTMENT OF NATURAL RESOURCES FOR HUNTING SEASONS AND REGULATIONS. INFORMATION IS AVAILABLE ON GAME AREA MAPS.

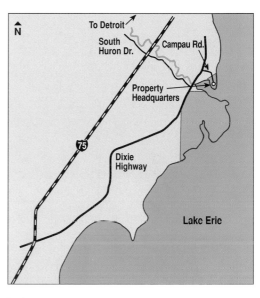

The great egret is one of southern Michigan's most elegant birds. Its dazzling white color is easily spotted in wetland habitats where it stalks for fish and frogs.

W. Perry Conway

Directions: From Detroit, take I-75 south to South Huron River Drive. Turn left (east) and proceed about 2 miles to a T intersection. Turn left at the T (Dixie Highway) and drive about 1/2 mile to Campau Road. Turn right onto Campau and follow the signs to the area headquarters.

Ownership: Michigan Department of Natural Resources (313) 379-9692

Size: 4,000 acres

Closest Towns: Rockwood, Gibraltar

The rough-legged hawk often hovers while searching for prey in the open fields and marshlands where it hunts.

Site Description: This site boasts nearly 3 miles of Lake Erie shoreline at the mouth of the Detroit River. Water is a major component of the habitat here, including lakes, ponds, river backwaters, and wetlands. Portions of this park are highly developed and receive heavy visitor traffic. However, its ideal location along Lake Erie makes this site home to some tremendous wildlife viewing opportunities.

Wildlife Viewing: Among wildlife watchers, this site is probably best known for its raptors, or birds-of-prey. During fall migration (September is best) it is possible to view more than 50,000 hawks here in a single day! Broad-winged hawks are the most numerous, and are often seen in kettles or groups of 3,000 or more. As many as 30,000 broad-wings may be seen on a given day. Be sure to bring your binoculars for a truly awe-inspiring sight. Lake Erie MetroPark is also very good for waterfowl viewing. Hot water from the Trenton power plant keeps a portion of the waterfront open throughout the winter, and this area is popular for ducks, geese, and swans. Bald eagles may also be seen fishing in this open water during winter.

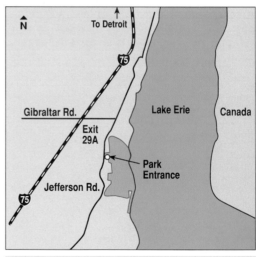

Directions: From Detroit, take I-75 south to Exit 29A (Gibraltar Road). Turn left (east) onto Gibraltar and proceed less than a mile to Jefferson Road. Turn right (south) onto Jefferson and continue to the park entrance on the left.

Ownership: Huron-Clinton Metropolitan Authority (313) 379-5020

Size: 1,600 acres

Closest Towns: Rockwood, Gibraltar

The double-crested cormorant is a goose-sized water bird that often perches upright (like a hawk or owl) on rocks or logs over the water.

Site Description: Metro Beach is a 750-acre peninsula that extends into Lake St. Clair. The park offers more than 7 miles of shoreline, 1,600 feet of boardwalk along the lake, and nature trails that explore a wetland in the park's interior. Trails have a wood chip base and are barrier free.

Wildlife Viewing: Metro Beach is excellent for watching birds. Birds that cross Lake St. Clair on their annual migrations use the park as a haven in which to rest and feed before continuing their journeys. During October, you may see tens of thousands of diving birds, including cormorants and loons, on a single day! In April and May you can view loons again as they migrate back north to their breeding grounds in northern Michigan and Canada. May also brings large numbers of warblers and other songbirds to the area. Least bitterns and black-crowned night herons have been seen and heard on the nature trails through the wetlands. At the end of August, watch for large groups of monarch butterflies and hummingbirds migrating to Mexico for the winter. Occasionally, snowy owls are seen here during winter.

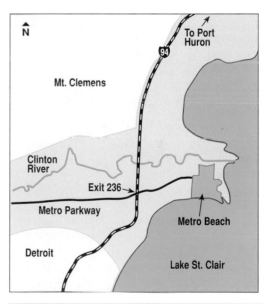

Directions: From Detroit, take I-94 east to Exit 236. Turn right onto Metro Parkway (16 Mile Road) and follow it about 3 miles to the park entrance.

Ownership: Huron-Clinton Metropolitan Authority (810) 463-4332

Size: 750 acres

Closest town: Mount Clemens

Site Description: This area boasts a diverse mixture of habitat types including glacier-formed lakes, wetlands, cedar swamps, prairie, and rolling woodlands. Five miles of hiking trails wind throughout all of these habitats. Boardwalks, bridges, and observation towers provide scenic views of the surrounding countryside and a close look at the wildlife that call these areas home.

Wildlife Viewing: Because Seven Ponds contains many different kinds of habitats, it is a good place to view wildlife throughout the year. The bird viewing can be especially rewarding, as more than 200 species have been sighted here. The list includes nesting bobolinks, bluebirds, tree swallows, and swamp sparrows. Good probability of viewing muskrats and beavers in the wetlands and lakes. Seven Ponds boasts a wonderful variety of wildflowers from spring through fall. The different habitats and seasons bring an ever-changing display of color to hill and dale. Excellent probability of seeing trilliums, yellow lady's slippers, jack-in-the-pulpits, and prairie coneflowers in proper season. Visit the nature center to discover what is currently in bloom. The nature center also has maps, interpretive materials, and a nice wildlife viewing/feeding window.

The yellow lady's slipper is one of Michigan's most beautiful wildflowers. This delicate orchid often grows in swamps, bogs, or forests with rich soils.

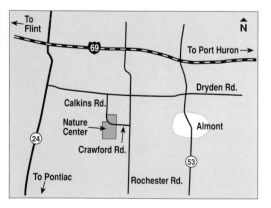

Directions: From the Detroit area, take M-53 north past Almont. Turn left onto Dryden Road. and proceed 7 miles to Calkins Road. Turn left onto Calkins and follow signs to the nature center.

Ownership: Michigan Audubon Society (810) 796-3200

Size: 273 acres

Closest town: Dryden

Site Description: This site contains nearly 100 acres of wild lands along the north branch of the Rouge River in suburban Troy. Habitats found here include cattail marsh, sedge meadow, lowland forest, rolling uplands, and beech-maple and oak-hickory forests. Almost two miles of trails dissect these diverse habitats. Stop at the nature center for a trail map and other materials. The nature center, restrooms, and some of the trails are barrier free.

Wildlife Viewing: Because of the many habitat types found here, this site offers a variety of unique plants and animals to observe. Wildflower viewing is excellent. From skunk cabbage that pushes up through February snow, to witch-hazel whose yellow blossoms add color to the forest long after autumn's leaves have fallen, wildflowers at this site are a real treasure. Nearly 200 kinds of birds may be seen here. Spring migration (April-May) is the best time for viewing. A bridge over the Rouge River near the nature center provides good fish viewing—bass, bluegill, and suckers are most common. Low areas along the river also are good for seeing herons, muskrats, painted turtles, and leopard frogs. The marsh tower on Fox Trail gives a very nice view of the Rouge River bottomlands.

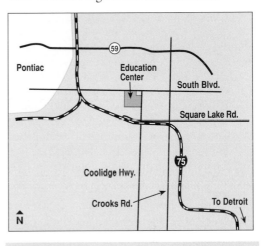

Directions: From Detroit, take I-75 north to Crooks Road Exit. Turn right (north) and proceed to Square Lake Road. Turn left (west) and continue to Coolidge Road. Turn right (north) and drive for 3/4 mile to the park entrance on the left.

Ownership: City of Troy (810) 524-3567

Size: 99 acres

Closest Town: Troy

The raccoon has become a common night-time visitor to most Michigan campsites. Raccoons are very adaptible to human development, so many urban residents have also become very familiar with this masked bandit.

Chris Doyal

Site Description: Though it's located in a bustling suburb only 20 miles from downtown Detroit, this beautiful area could easily be mistaken for northern Michigan. Tall, steep hills covered with stately oak and hickory trees lead down into bottomland forest and wetland areas. The nature preserve is also the western trailhead of the West Bloomfield Trail Network, a 4.25-mile abandoned railroad corridor that has been converted to a linear greenway. The entire greenway is barrier free. Bicycles are allowed on the trail network only.

Wildlife Viewing: The primary attraction of this site is the active heron rookery which is plainly visible from the west end of the greenway trail. More than 200 great blue herons nest in flooded hardwood forest. Courtship begins in March, and nesting activity continues until the young leave the nest in August. A 2.5-mile trail (1/2 mile of which is barrier free) wanders through the hills and valleys of the nature preserve, offering fair-to-good opportunities to view squirrels, rabbits, raccoons, frogs, toads, and woodland wildflowers.

Directions: From Detroit, drive north on I-75 to I-696. Take I-696 west to the Orchard Lake Road exit. Turn north and drive about 6 miles to Pontiac Trail. Turn left (west) and continue about 1.5 miles to Arrowhead Road. Turn left (south) and proceed about 1/2 mile to the park entrance on the left.

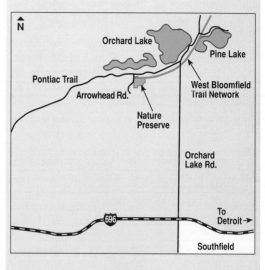

Ownership: West Bloomfield Parks and Recreation Commission (810) 334-5660.

Size: 162 acres

Closest Town: West Bloomfield

Wooden overlooks along the West Bloomfield Trail Network provide good views of the wetlands in the adjoining nature preserve. Great blue herons nest in these flooded trees.

Phil T. Seng

Site Description: Located at the headwaters of the Clinton River, Independence Oaks contains the full spectrum of habitat types; from dry, upland forest, to fallow farm fields, to river floodplains, to a 68-acre lake. Nearly 10 miles of trails wander about through these diverse habitats.

Wildlife Viewing: An extensive bluebird trail that runs through the fallow farm fields and open areas of the park offers a good probability of viewing bluebirds and tree swallows from March through August. Overall, more than 150 species of birds have been sighted here. Stop at the nature center to pick up a bird checklist and other materials. A feeding station at the nature center attracts many of the small mammals and songbirds that do not migrate to warmer climates for the winter. On the lake, turtles and water snakes are plentiful, and the river floodplain area is a good location to look for the small, reclusive massasauga rattlesnake. Massasaugas are poisonous but non-aggressive. If you find one, observe it from a healthy distance and count yourself as one of the lucky few who ever see Michigan's only rattlesnake.

The bullfrog is Michigan's largest frog. Although their diet consists primarily of insects, large bullfrogs have been known to eat mice, bats, and even ducklings!

Directions: Take I-75 north out of Detroit. Exit at Sashabaw Road near Clarkston. Turn right (north) and and travel 2 miles past Pine Knob Music Theater. Park entrance is on the left side of the road.

Ownership: Oakland County Parks and Recreation Commission (810) 625-6473 or 625-0877

Size: 1,088 acres

Closest Town: Clarkston

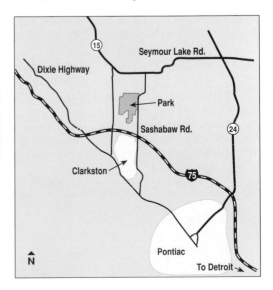

Michael M. Smith

The fringed gentian is one of the last Michigan wildflowers to bloom in late summer. These showy blossoms open to the sun and then close up again at night and on cloudy days.

also be seen from the trails at dawn and dusk. Wildflower viewing is fantastic here. From mid-April through June, look for the intricate blossoms of showy lady's slippers, trout lilies, trilliums, and other wildflowers in the nature study area. Two carnivorous or meat-eating plants—the sundew and the pitcher plant—are common in the bog area near Timberland Lake. These unusual plants trap and digest insects to help them survive in the nutrient-poor bog habitat. Please do not pick or damage plants in this fragile wetland community.

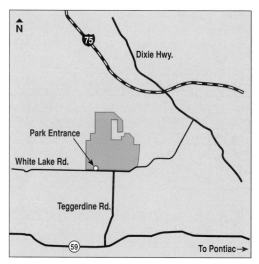

Site Description: Located in the headwaters of the Huron River, this park preserves a large piece of the Huron Swamp. The majority of the habitat here is marshland and swamp forest, but there also are meadows, brushy old fields, and upland forests. An 8-mile, barrier-free, hike-bike trail shows visitors a beautiful cross-section of Indian Springs, while a 6-mile network of hiking trails waits for those who want to explore individual habitats a little closer. Stop at the nature center for a map of the trail system and other materials.

Wildlife Viewing: Excellent probability of viewing common wetland wildlife such as muskrats, herons, and wood ducks almost anywhere along the trail system. Deer may

Directions: From Pontiac, take M-59 to Teggerdine Road. Turn right (north) and proceed to White Lake Road. Turn left (west) and continue about 1 mile to the park entrance on the right.

Ownership: Huron-Clinton Metropolitan Authority (810) 625-7280

Size: 2,232 acres

Closest Town: Pontiac

White-tailed deer fawns produce no scent, so when they remain motionless they do not attract predators. The coloration of their coats imitates the partial sunlight that filters through the treetops onto the brown forest floor.

in trees on the small island in Wildwing Lake. It's easiest to see these large wading birds in April and early May. Kensington is also home to nearly 400 kinds of wild-flowers.

DO NOT FEED THE DEER. IT MAY RESULT IN THEIR INJURY OR DEATH. SEE THE SECTION ON FEEDING WILD ANIMALS IN THE FRONT OF THIS BOOK FOR MORE INFORMATION.

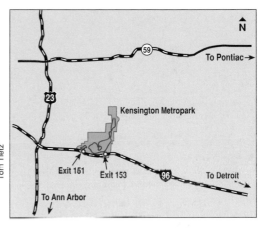

Site Description: More than 1,200 acres of water are nestled among the rolling, wooded hills of Kensington Metropark. Part of this park is highly developed and highly used, but the nature study area has been tailored for wildlife viewing. Miles of hiking trails radiate from the nature center throughout the wetlands, forests, and fields of this site.

Wildlife Viewing: If you like viewing white-tailed deer, this is the place to come. Deer are very likely to be observed during any season or time of day. Look for them in open areas along park roads—Route 2 is especially good. For a more natural experience, stalk quietly along the nature trails in the morning or evening. The scarlet tanager and Acadian flycatcher are two of the 247 bird species that have been identified within Kensington. Great blue herons have nested

Directions: From Detroit, take I-96 west to Exit 151 or Exit 153. Large signs at both exits direct you to park entrances.

Ownership: Huron-Clinton Metropolitan Authority (810) 227-2757 or 685-1561

Size: 4,337 acres

Closest Towns: Milford, Brighton

Site Description: This combination of federal, state, and local natural areas conserves a wonderful complex of river wetlands located just outside of Saginaw. Rivers and streams that come together here drain a total of 22 different counties—the largest watershed in Michigan. Wetlands and backwaters of Flint, the Shiawassee, Tittabawassee, and Cass rivers, provide fantastic habitats for a variety of wetland wildlife. LARGE NUMBERS OF MOSQUITOES ARE COMMON HERE DURING SPRING AND EARLY SUMMER.

Ron Austing

Huge concentrations of ducks and geese descend on wetlands along the Shiawassee River during their spring and fall migration. The Shiawassee National Wildlife Refuge alone may host more than 50,000 waterfowl at a time!

Wildlife Viewing at Shiawassee National Wildlife Refuge: This site is home to some incredible waterfowl viewing. There is a good probability of seeing ducks and geese any time of the year, but during March/April and again in October/November, numbers of these birds may be spectacular. It is not uncommon for the refuge to host more than 30,000 ducks and an additional 25,000 geese as they travel between their breeding areas in the North and their wintering areas in the South. This site has been named one of the top 25 birding sites in America. Prothonotary warblers and brown creepers are but two of the interesting birds that spend time at the refuge. The Woodland and Ferguson Bayou hiking trails wind among bottomland hardwood forest and wetland areas. An observation tower complete with a 10-power spotting scope along the Ferguson Bayou trail provides a great view of wildlife in the wetlands and bald eagles that like to perch along the river. Bicycling and skiing are allowed along the designated trail systems. Trails are open dawn to dusk year-round, except during the hunting season. TRAILS MAY FLOOD DURING TIMES OF HIGH WATER. Stop at the refuge headquarters for maps and other materials and to determine trail availability during

autumn. Restroom facilities are limited on the refuge.

Facilities at the National Wildlife Refuge:

Wildlife Viewing at Shiawassee River State Game Area: High probability of viewing ducks, geese, and swans throughout the year. Huge concentrations of geese are common in the spring and fall. Mallards, black ducks, and wood ducks are the most common ducks seen here. High probability of seeing white-tailed deer any time of year. Walk any of the dikes and access roads to get a closer look at the abundant wildlife found at this large site. Camping is prohibited from April 1 - December 31.

Facilities at the State Game Area:

Wildlife Viewing at Green Point Environmental Learning Center: Because of its location along the Tittabawassee River corridor in Saginaw, this site is very attractive to many migrating songbirds. Birds that migrate along the river tend to congregate here to rest and feed before continuing their journeys. Mid-May is

Facilities at Green Point:

Red-tailed hawks nest in the tall trees and hunt in the open areas surrounding the Shiawassee River bottoms. They are often seen soaring in broad, lazy circles or perching on posts or trees along roadways.

W. Perry Conway

TRAILS MAY FLOOD DURING TIMES OF HEAVY RAIN. PORTIONS OF THE NATIONAL WILDLIFE REFUGE AND ALL OF THE STATE GAME AREA ARE OPEN TO PUBLIC HUNTING. CONTACT THE SITE MANAGERS FOR HUNTING SEASONS AND REGULATIONS. HUNTING IS NOT PERMITTED AT GREEN POINT ENVIRONMENTAL LEARNING CENTER.

Directions To National Wildlife Refuge Headquarters: From Saginaw, take M-13 south about 5 miles to Curtis Road, turn right (west) and proceed less than 1 mile to the refuge headquarters.

To Shiawassee State Game Area Headquarters: From Saginaw, take M-46 west to M-52. Turn left (south) and proceed about 8 miles to the St. Charles Field Office on the left side of the road.

To Green Point Environmental Learning Center: From M-46 in Saginaw, take Michigan Avenue south to Maple Street. Turn left onto Maple and proceed to the nature center parking lot on the right.

Ownership: Shiawassee National Wildlife Refuge: U.S. Fish and Wildlife Service (517) 777-5930

Shiawassee River State Game Area: Michigan Department of Natural Resources (517) 865-6211

Green Point Nature Center: City of Saginaw (517) 759-1669

Size: Shiawassee National Wildlife Refuge: 9,000 acres

Shiawassee River State Game Area: 8,490 acres

Green Point Environmental Learning Center: 82 acres

Closest Towns: Saginaw, St. Charles

the peak of the spring warbler migration. Overall, nearly 150 different kinds of birds may be seen at Green Point during the year. More than 2 miles of hiking trails explore the mixed hardwood and bottomland forest. There are 40 tree species found here and some of the individual trees are very old, providing good nesting habitat for squirrels, woodpeckers, and wood ducks. Green Point Environmental Learning Center is owned by the City of Saginaw but operated through a cooperative agreement with the U.S. Fish and Wildlife Service. The Center has a wildlife viewing room that provides good opportunities for visitors to view songbirds, small mammals, and other wildlife at several feeding stations.

143

Night Species

Michigan has some extremely interesting animals that are active only at night. Some of these animals are fairly common, but most people rarely see them. Although wildlife viewing after dark is challenging, you can be successful with a little knowledge and a lot of practice.

Bats

Bats are the only mammals that truly fly. Their bodies are covered with fur, but their wings are naked and nearly transparent. They have a distinctive fluttering appearance when seen in flight. Watch for bats around wetland areas where they often gather to feed.

Owls

From the 8" saw-whet to the 30" great gray, Michigan's owls may be best recognized by their erect postures and large heads and eyes. Some have large ear tufts but some—like the barred owl pictured—do not. During the day, owls perch motionless in trees. At dusk, look for them along field borders and listen for their distinctive hooting calls.

Skunks

Most people recognize the distinctive colors (and smell) of the skunk, even if they have never seen a live one. Adults are about 2 feet long and spend their time on the ground in mixed forest and open areas.

Flying Squirrels

Flying squirrels are the smallest Michigan squirrels, less than a foot in length (including the 5-inch tail). They have extremely soft, loose fur that is brown or gray on top and white underneath. Though fairly common, they are shy and rarely seen.

Opossums

The Virginia opossum—North America's only marsupial—is about the size of a large house cat. It is easily recognized by its white face and large, rounded ears. The foot-long tail is pinkish and naked and can be used for grasping and climbing.

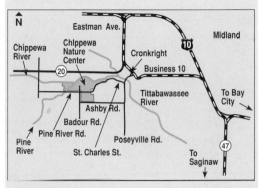

Site Description: Chippewa Nature Center contains a network of interpretive trails that meander through wetlands, lowland forest, and upland meadows at the confluence of the Pine and Chippewa Rivers. Learn about the wildlife and history of the area at the extensive visitor center and museum. Be sure to stop at the viewing window that overlooks the river. This 890-acre site also contains ponds, an abandoned river oxbow wetland, and an arboretum of native Michigan trees and shrubs. The visitor center is barrier free.

Wildlife Viewing: This area provides an excellent look at the wildlife associated with riparian (river) corridors. Watch for beavers and muskrats at dawn and dusk in the ponds, wetlands, and rivers. Fair to good probability of seeing kingfishers fishing along the river. These blue jay-size water birds dive head-first into the water to catch the small fish that make up most of their diet. Racoons are common at dawn and dusk. Huge old trees can be seen near the oxbow. Deer, woodchucks, and chipmunks are plentiful throughout the area. Stop at the visitor center to pick up an area map and other materials.

Directions: Follow US-10 into Midland. Exit onto Business Route 10 and follow it to Poseyville Road from Cronkright Street. Turn southwest onto Poseyville and cross the bridge. Immediately turn right onto St. Charles Street and follow the signs about 3 miles to the nature center.

Ownership: Chippewa Nature Center, Inc. (517) 631-0830

Size: 890 acres

Closest Town: Midland

When threatened, opossums often hiss and bare their teeth in an effort to bluff the attacker. If this doesn't work, they may actually lose consciousness or "play dead." This strategy works well on some predators, but it is not very successful on the highway.

Site Description: Tobico is one of the largest open-water marshes remaining on the Saginaw Bay, but this area contains much more than just the marsh. On a short hike you can traverse several different types of habitats; from cattail marsh, to brushy shrub areas, to upland hardwood forest. The shoreline is layered with sandy dune ridges which once were at the water's edge, but were left high and dry as the Bay receded over thousands of years. A boardwalk and two large observation towers offer excellent wildlife viewing along the Frank N. Andersen Trail.

Gijsbert van Frankenhuyzen

Caspian terns are solitary birds that rarely gather in groups except to form small breeding colonies. They prefer to nest on the sandy shores of small islands.

Wildlife Viewing: Good probability of seeing waterfowl and shorebirds almost year round. Watch for caspian terns and black-crowned night herons which are very common here. In May, you may see pike and carp spawning in the open water around the bridges and boardwalks along the trail. This area is an excellent funnel for migrating warblers in the spring. Spend some time on the two observation towers to get a bird's-eye view into the surrounding tree tops. White-tailed deer are occasionally seen in the early morning—especially at the northern end of the trail.

HUNTING IS PROHIBITED ON TOBICO MARSH, BUT IS PERMITTED ON SOME OF THE OUTLYING AREAS. SEE A PROPERTY MAP FOR DETAILS.

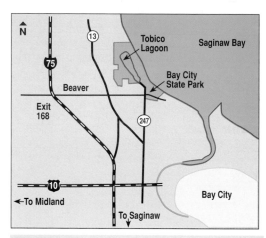

Directions: From I-75, take Exit 168 (Beaver Road) and drive east 5 miles to the entrance of Bay City State Park. Turn left into the day use area of the park, and park at the Jennison Nature Center. Stop at the nature center for a map of the area. The entrance to the Frank N. Andersen Trail is located just outside the nature center.

Ownership: Michigan Department of Natural Resources (517) 667-0717

Size: 2,000 acres

Closest Town: Bay City

   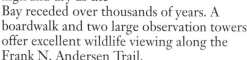

The large, majestic snowy owl is a bird of the far North that occasionally wanders south into Michigan when winter food is scarce.

W. Perry Conway

to see wildlife in and around the refuge. Drive the county roads to view birds feeding in local farm fields and wetlands. Drive north on Ringle Road to view the tip of Fish Point and Saginaw Bay. Several private lodges here cater to wildlife watchers and sportsmen. During winter, it is not uncommon to see snowy owls at Fish Point. These large, majestic owls normally do not spend much time in lower Michigan, but when the food is scarce in their northern homelands, they may drift south to try their luck.

PORTIONS OF THIS AREA ARE OPEN TO PUBLIC HUNTING. CHECK WITH THE MICHIGAN DEPARTMENT OF NATURAL RESOURCES FOR HUNTING SEASONS AND REGULATIONS.

Directions: From Unionville, follow M-25 west for 3 miles to Ringle Road. Turn right (north) and proceed 3 miles to the property boundary.

Site Description: The thumb region of Michigan is known for being flat, and Fish Point is no exception. This site contains more than 3,000 acres of flat farm fields, diked floodings, and coastal wetlands. Biologists manage water levels and vegetation for the benefit of waterfowl and other animals that rely on wetland habitats for survival.

Wildlife Viewing: Because of the tremendous variety and abundance of waterfowl found here, the Fish Point area has been called the "Chesapeake of the Midwest." During spring migration (March-April) the habitat and food resources at this site attract thousands of ducks and other water birds. PART OF THE STATE GAME AREA IS A WILDLIFE REFUGE. THE REFUGE IS OFF-LIMITS TO THE PUBLIC YEAR-ROUND. An observation tower and wildlife viewing trail provide excellent opportunities

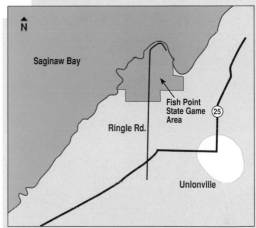

Ownership: Michigan Department of Natural Resources (517) 674-2511

Size: 3,200 acres

Closest Town: Unionville

Indian pipes are unique plants that contain no chlorophyll, meaning they have no green color and cannot make their own food. Instead, they get nourishment from decaying organic matter on the forest floor.

plants that like to have their "feet wet." There aren't many other places in nature where plants with totally different strategies for surviving can successfully coexist within a few feet of each other. Other interesting plants found here include pink lady's slipper (see hundreds during May), trailing arbutus, Indian pipes, jack-in-the-pulpit, and wintergreen. In addition to the interesting plant life, look for deer, squirrels, and hognose snakes. The spring warbler migration is also quite good.

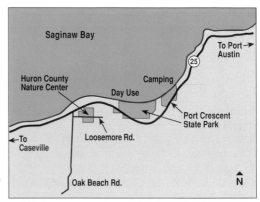

Site Description: Located less than a mile from the shores of Saginaw Bay, this 280-acre nature center is a wonderful example of undisturbed dune and swale habitat. A network of trails snakes atop dry, gently-rolling dune ridges and down into shallow, wet depressions known as swales. An interpretive display for the trail system and other educational materials are in production. Restrooms, a visitor center, and camping facilities are planned for the future.

Wildlife Viewing: This site is home to some very interesting and unique plant communities. The dry, sandy ridges are ruled by jack pine, black oak, and bracken fern—all of which are adapted to living in barren, dry conditions. But down in the moist swales things are different. Mosses, sedges, and red maples dominate here, and these are all

Directions: From Caseville, take M-25 east about 9 miles to Oak Beach Road. Turn right (south) and drive to Loosemore Road. Turn left (east) on Loosemore and continue to the park entrance on the left.

Ownership: Huron County Nature Center Wilderness Arboretum (517) 269-6431 or 1-800-35-THUMB

Size: 280 acres

Closest Town: Port Austin

Site Description: Located near the tip of Michigan's thumb region, Port Crescent State Park encompasses 3 miles of Lake Huron beachfront, sand dunes, dune forest, and backwaters and bayous of the Pinnebog River.

Wildlife Viewing: This site is an excellent destination for viewing the spring hawk migration. From March through April, broad-winged hawks and other birds-of-prey congregate here to rest and feed before continuing their journey to northern breeding grounds. At times you can view large kettles or groups of these birds soaring upon the drafts of air that come across Lake Huron and are funneled upward by the dune ridges. Loons also migrate through this area in April, and large concentrations of bluebirds bring color and character to the fields near the park entrance.

PORTIONS OF THIS AREA ARE OPEN TO PUBLIC HUNTING. CHECK WITH THE MICHIGAN DEPARTMENT OF NATURAL RESOURCES FOR HUNTING SEASONS AND REGULATIONS.

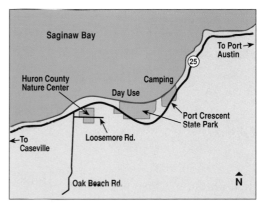

Directions: From Port Austin, take M-25 west about 5 miles to the Port Crescent campground entrance. Continue west on M-25 another 2 miles to the day use entrance.

Ownership: Michigan Department of Natural Resources (517) 738-8663

Size: 565 acres

Closest Town: Port Austin

A wild turkey gobbler struts and "puffs up" to impress hens during the spring mating season.

Other Wildlife Viewing Sites in the Southern Lower Peninsula

	Site Name	County	Phone Number
1.	Saugatuck Dunes State Park	Allegan	616-399-9390
2.	Nayanguing Point	Bay	517-697-5101
3.	Warren Dunes State Park	Berrien	616-426-4013
4.	Battle Creek Linear Park	Calhoun	616-966-3431
5.	Bernard Baker Sanctuary	Calhoun	517-886-9144
6.	Edward Keenhe Environmental Center	Eaton	517-627-7351
7.	Grand Blanc Commons	Genesee	810-694-1118
8.	Somerset State Game Area	Hillsdale	517-780-7904
9.	Rush Lake State Game Area	Huron	517-269-6431
10.	Wild Fowl Bay State Game Area	Huron	517-872-5300
11.	Fenner Arboretum	Ingham	517-483-4224
12.	Island Lake Recreation Area	Livingston	810-229-7067
13.	Stony Creek Metropark	Macomb	810-781-4621
14.	Sterling State Park	Monroe	313-289-2715
15.	White River Trail	Muskegon	616-894-4048
16.	Gunnar Mettala Park	Oakland	810-624-2850
17.	Highland Recreation Area	Oakland	810-887-5135
18.	Holly Recreation Area	Oakland	810-634-0240
19.	Window on the Waterfront	Ottawa	616-392-9044
20.	Van Raalte Farm	Ottawa	616-392-9044
21.	East Grand River Park	Ottawa	616-842-3210
22.	Harsens Island Wildlife Area	St. Clair	810-748-9504
23.	St. John's Marsh Wildlife Area	St. Clair	810-748-9504
24.	Wilderness Park	Washtenaw	313-429-4907
25.	Furstenberg Park	Washtenaw	313-994-2780
26.	Hudson Mills Metropark	Washtenaw	313-426-8211
27.	Dolph Park	Washtenaw	313-994-2780
28.	Pinckney Recreation Area	Washtenaw	313-426-4913
29.	Matthaei Botanical Gardens	Washtenaw	313-998-7061
30.	Downtown Detroit	Wayne	313-953-0241

Wildlife Index

Following are some of Michigan's most popular wildlife species and some of the best places to find them. Remember that the site numbers listed here are only some of the locations these animals are found—most can be viewed at other sites as well.

Species	Site Numbers
Bats	7
Bald eagles	5, 22, 25, 29, 41, 55, 61, 68, 72, 76, 102, 116
Beavers	1, 2, 10, 19, 27, 34, 43, 49, 63, 67, 84, 110
Black bears	2, 10, 13, 15, 17, 29
Bluebirds	87, 91, 94, 99, 110, 113, 121
Butterflies	23, 39, 71, 94, 98, 109
Geese	14, 21, 38, 57, 62, 70, 77, 86, 96, 102, 116
Cormorants	16, 20, 109
Deer	9, 16, 19, 29, 57, 60, 70, 84, 86, 95, 106, 114, 115
Egrets	37, 47, 52, 57, 80, 104
Elk	56
Fish	16, 41, 45, 83, 90, 93, 98, 111
Foxes	1, 10, 13, 17, 50, 84, 87, 89
Grouse	10, 15, 33, 51, 60, 67, 76, 95, 100
Hawks	2, 12, 13, 25, 33, 39, 44, 60, 81, 86, 94, 108, 121
Herons	5, 20, 23, 38, 49, 57, 62, 70, 80, 102, 112, 114, 118
Kingfishers	4, 21, 58, 64, 98, 117
Loons	1, 6, 20, 29, 33, 54, 55, 63, 65, 69, 75, 90, 109
Muskrats	11, 19, 42, 43, 61, 62, 97, 110, 114
Ospreys	14, 22, 29, 34, 40, 41, 43, 57, 61, 75, 102
Otters	2, 8, 10, 29, 32, 41, 44, 48, 61, 62, 65, 76
Owls	33, 48, 50, 60, 82, 109, 119
Peregrine falcons	2, 13
Woodpeckers	6, 13, 15, 39, 50, 59, 75, 76, 81, 106, 116
Sandhill cranes	11, 29, 95, 103, 105
Shorebirds	9, 14, 23, 24, 33, 62, 70, 78, 107, 118
Snakes	47, 81, 91, 94, 97, 100, 113, 120
Trumpeter swans	29, 69, 96
Turkeys	21, 46, 57, 95, 100, 104
Turtles	19, 42, 49, 58, 72, 94, 97, 111, 113
Warblers	6, 23, 26, 32, 44, 66, 67, 75, 85, 109, 116, 120
Wildflowers	1, 31, 44, 53, 69, 88, 92, 110, 111, 114, 115
Wood ducks	11, 21, 75, 88, 114, 116

David Kenyon

Since 1983 Michigan taxpayers have had the opportunity to support programs involving endangered and nongame wildlife through donations on their income tax form. These voluntary contributions have helped:

- Reintroduce peregrine falcons and trumpeter swans
- Print and distribute over 2 million educational posters
- Complete a statewide breeding bird census
- Protect a major bat hibernation site
- Construct numerous boardwalks and observation platforms

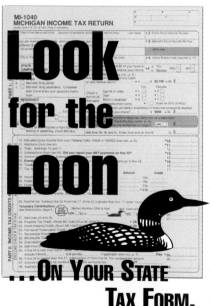

Citizens in all 83 Michigan counties have been touched in some way by contributions to the nongame wildlife fund.

In addition, the nongame fund has distributed small grants to universities, organizations, and individuals for specific nongame projects. Grants have funded construction of school site learning centers and banding of eagles. They have also supported important research on species including saw-whet owls, karner blue butterflies, massasauga rattlesnakes, and pine martens.

The *Michigan Wildlife Viewing Guide* is just one more project to enhance your knowledge and enjoyment of our precious natural resources. You can help. Direct donations can be made to:

MDNR - Wildlife Division, Nongame Wildlife Fund
Dept. WW
P.O. Box 30180
Lansing, Michigan 48909-7680